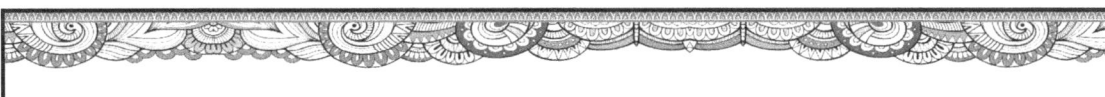

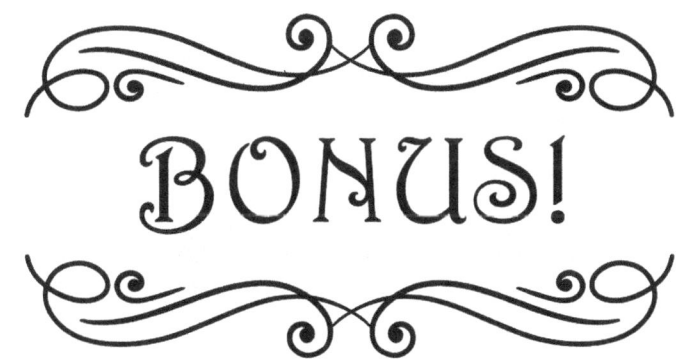

BONUS!

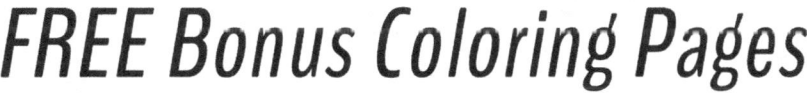

FREE Bonus Coloring Pages

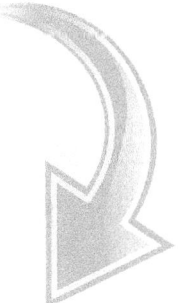

www.AmazingColorArt.com/bonus

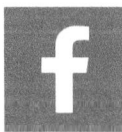 FB.com/AmazingColorArt

 @amazingcolorart

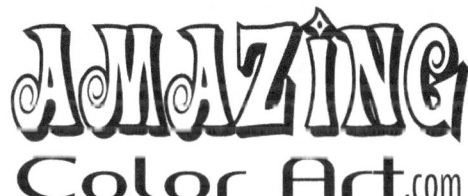
AMAZING Color Art.com

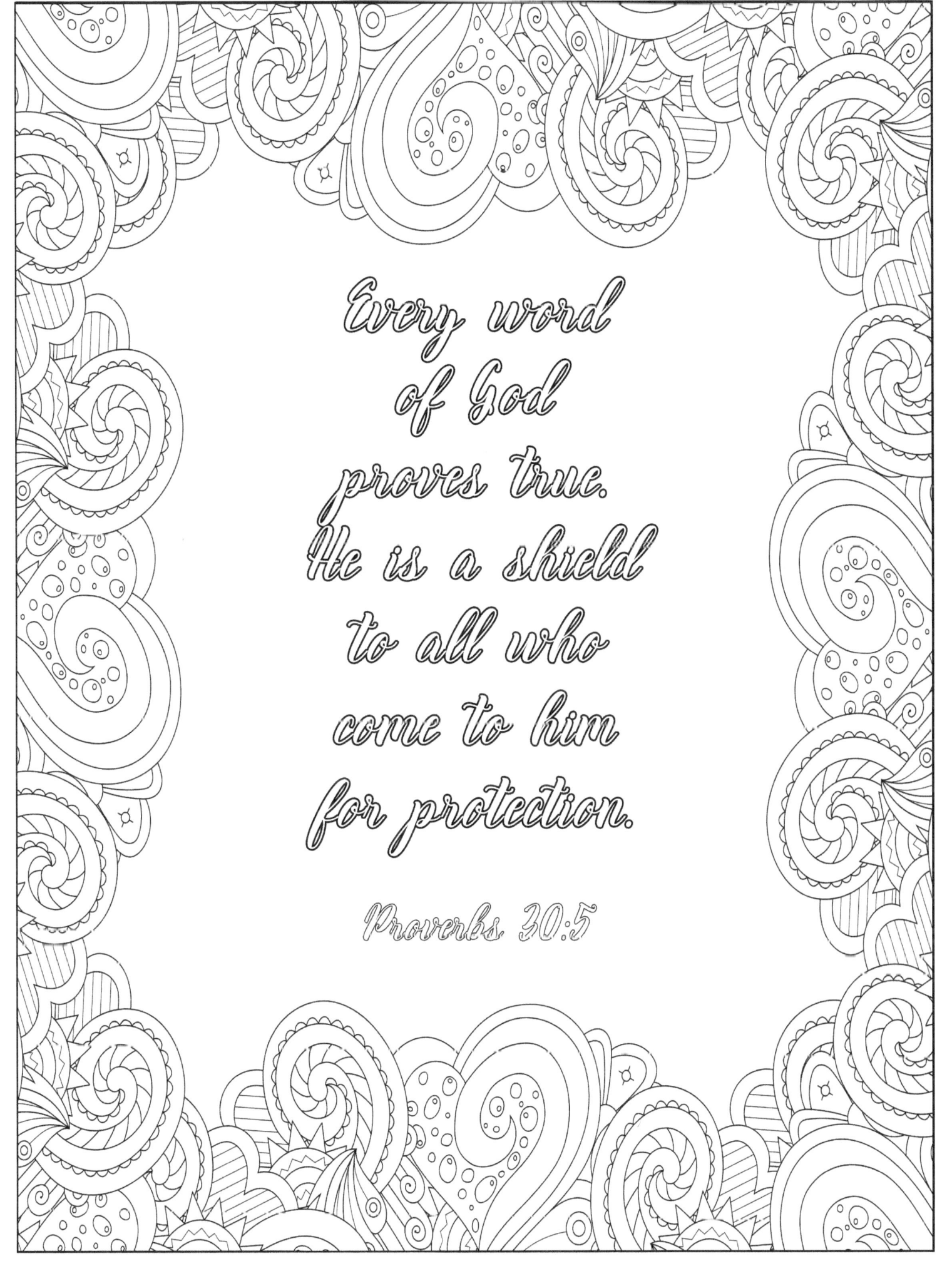

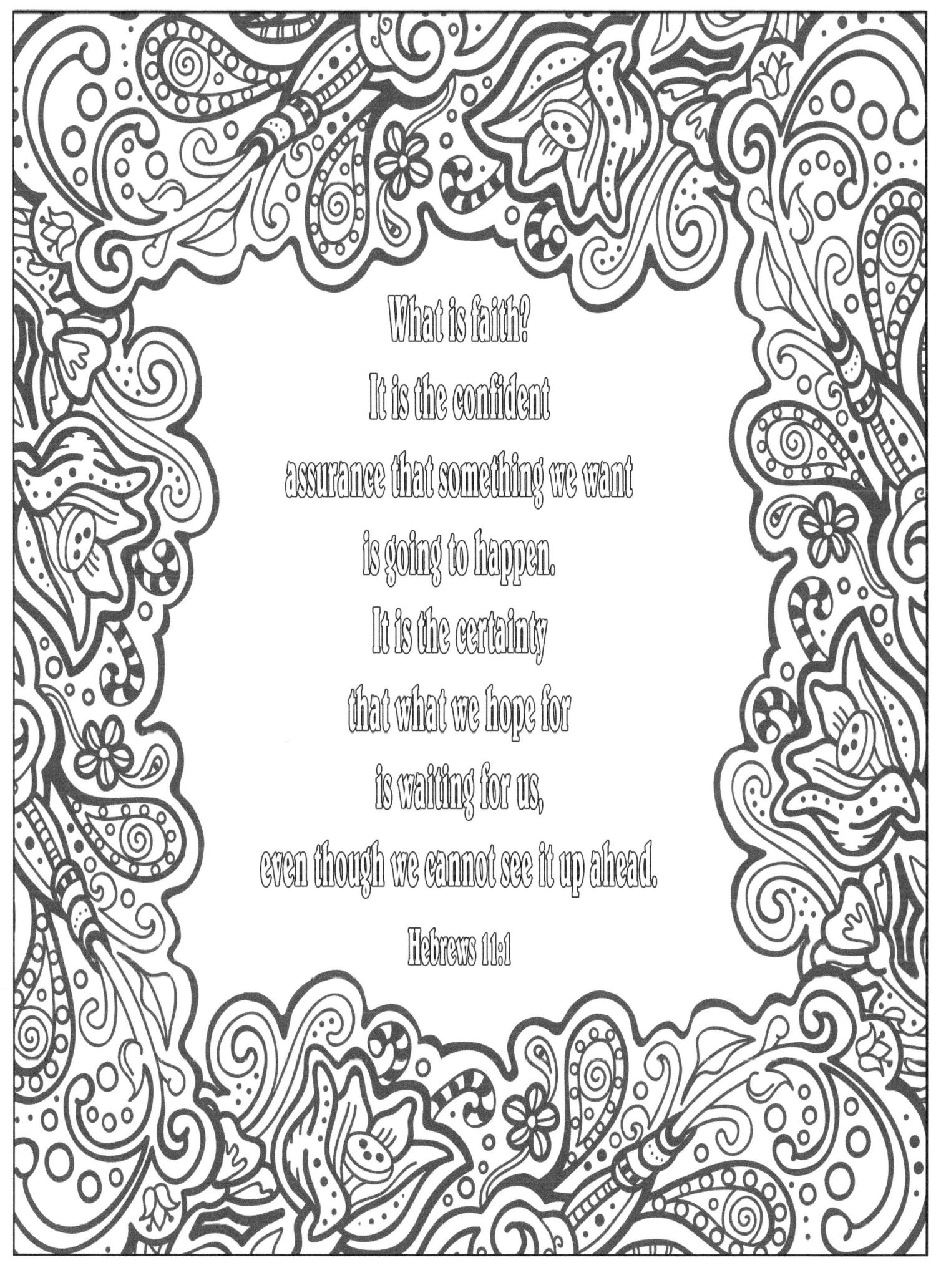

What is faith?
It is the confident
assurance that something we want
is going to happen.
It is the certainty
that what we hope for
is waiting for us,
even though we cannot see it up ahead.

Hebrews 11:1

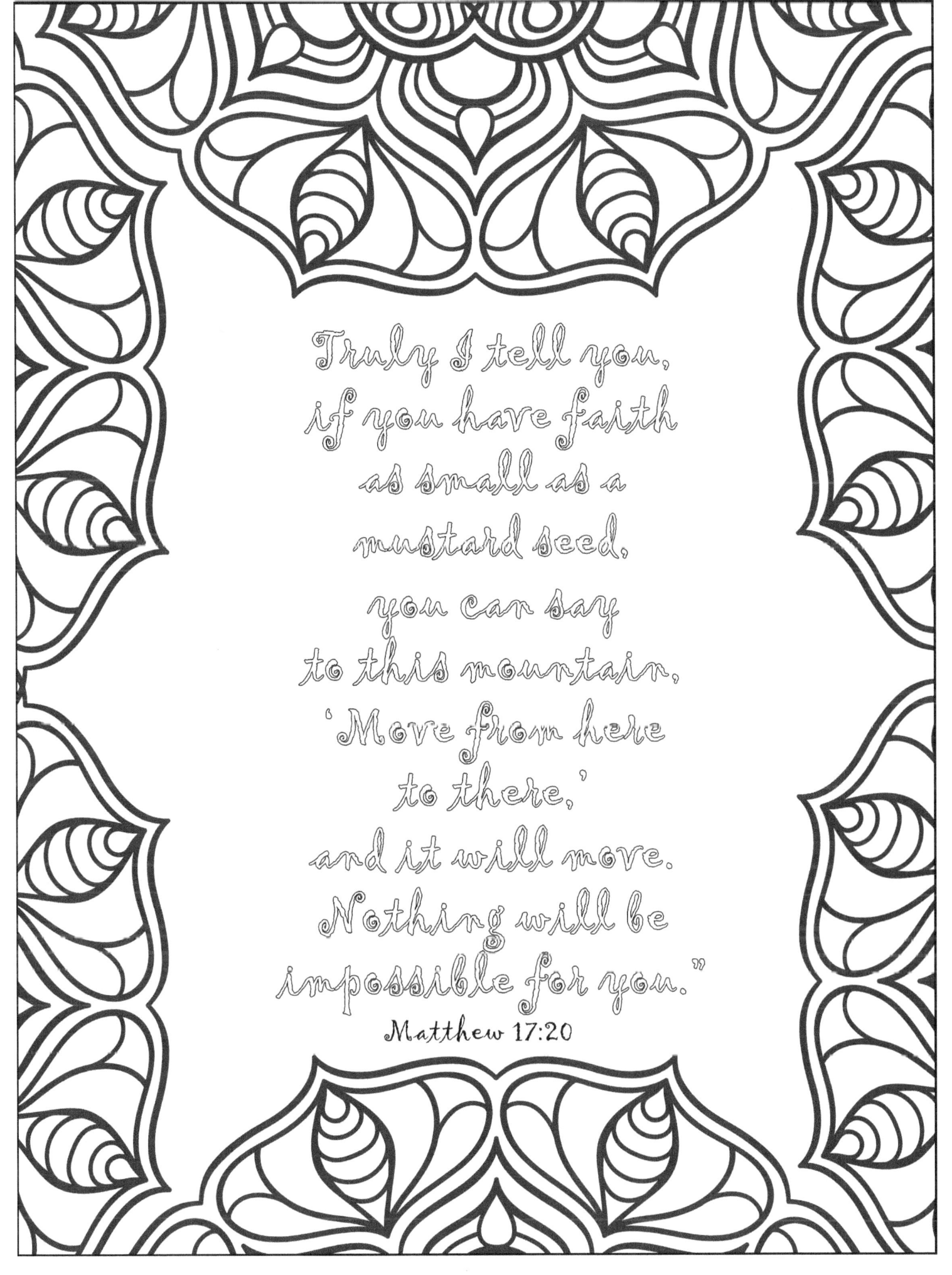

Truly I tell you,
if you have faith
as small as a
mustard seed,
you can say
to this mountain,
'Move from here
to there,'
and it will move.
Nothing will be
impossible for you."

Matthew 17:20

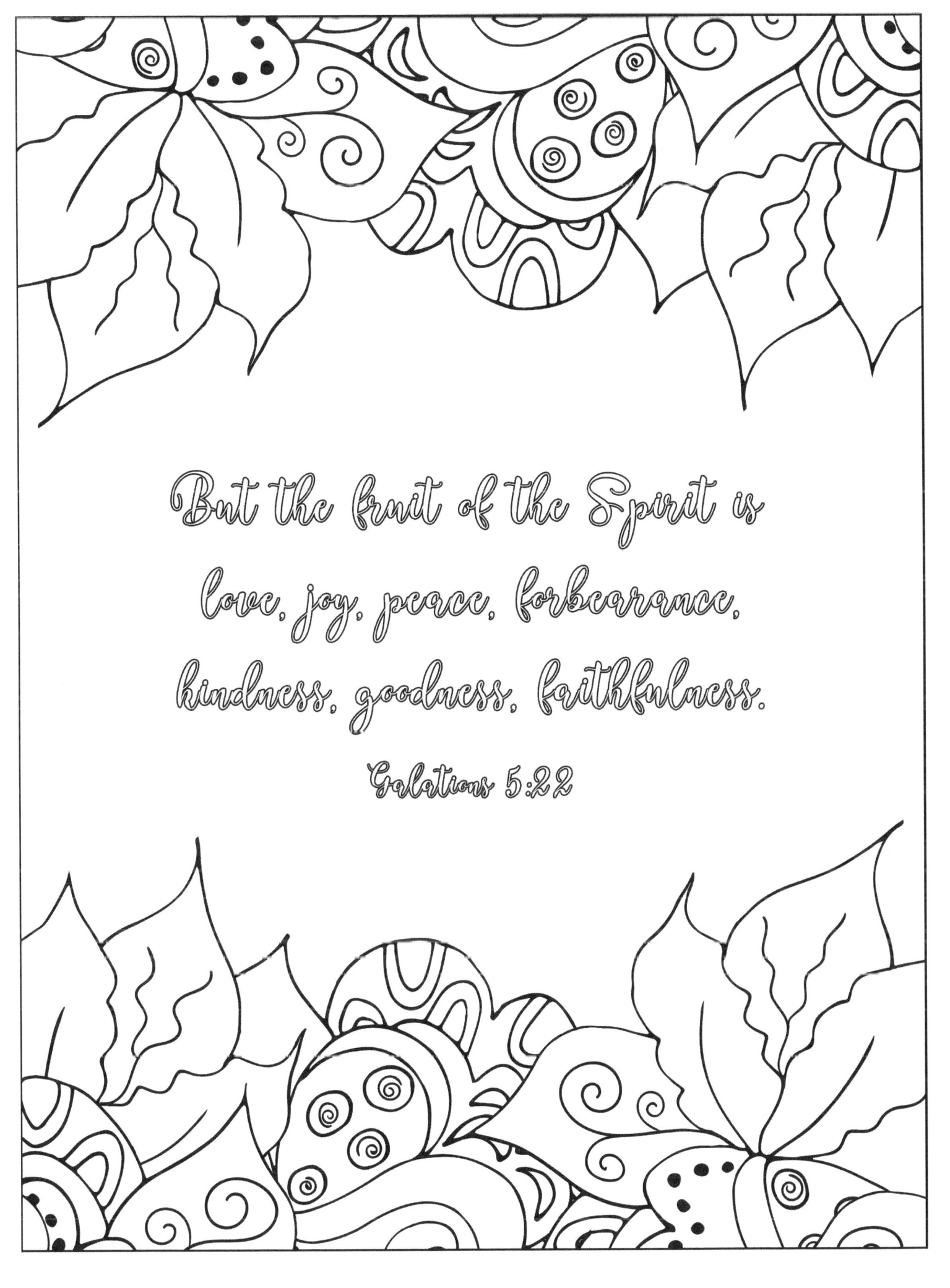

But the fruit of the Spirit is
love, joy, peace, forbearance,
kindness, goodness, faithfulness.

Galatians 5:22

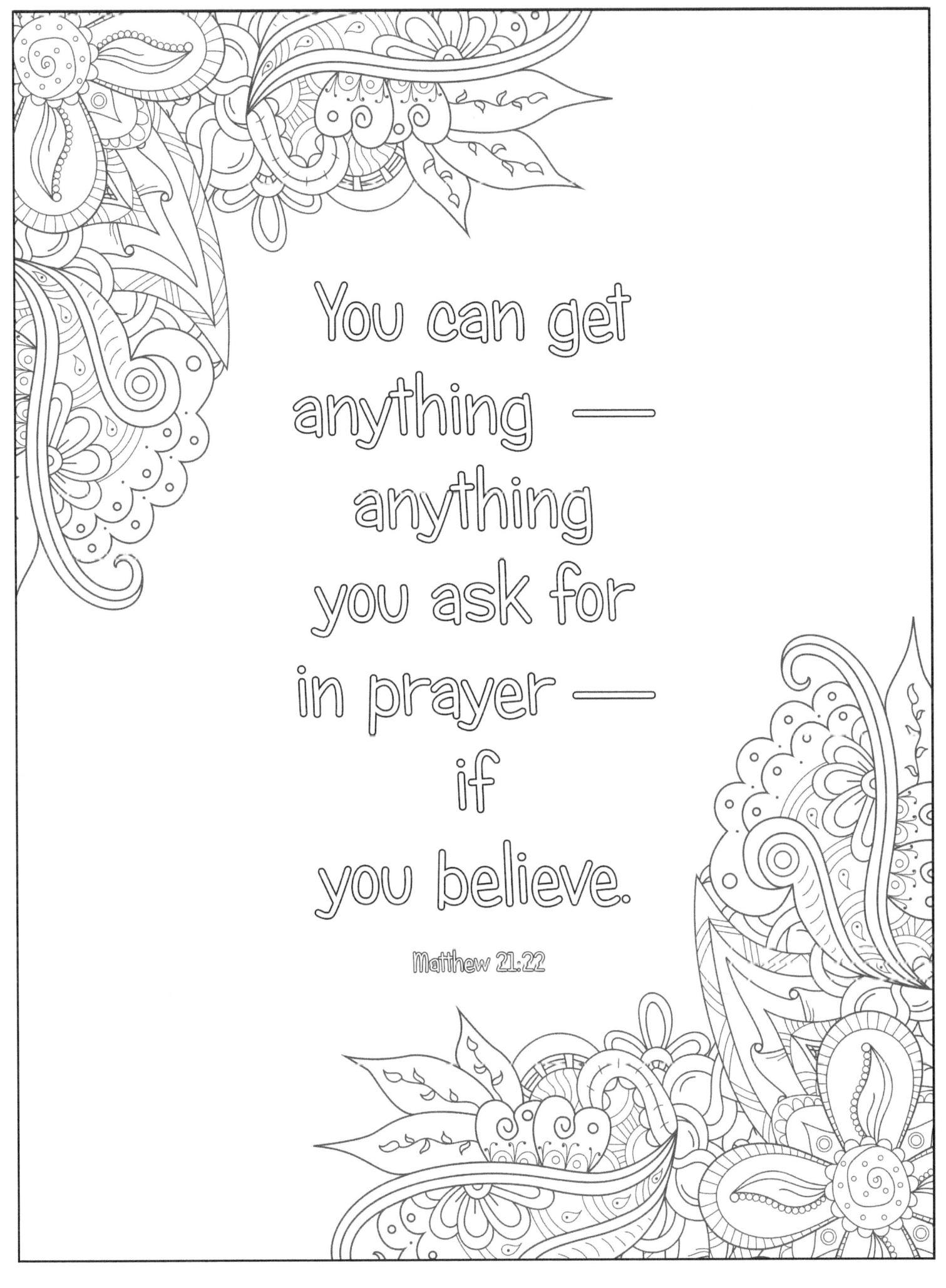

You can get
anything —
anything
you ask for
in prayer —
if
you believe.

Matthew 21:22

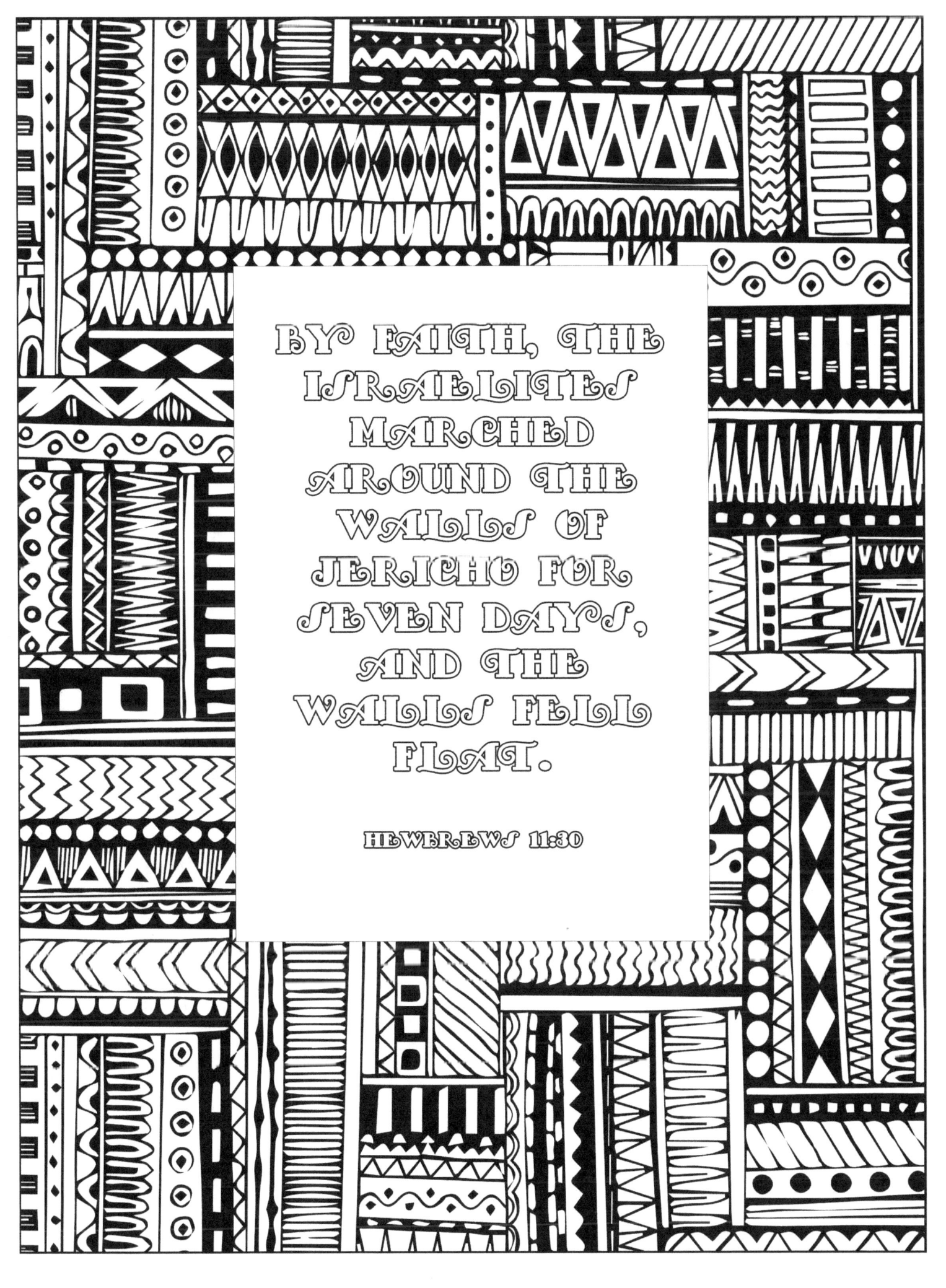

BY FAITH, THE ISRAELITES MARCHED AROUND THE WALLS OF JERICHO FOR SEVEN DAYS, AND THE WALLS FELL FLAT.

HEWBREWS 11:30

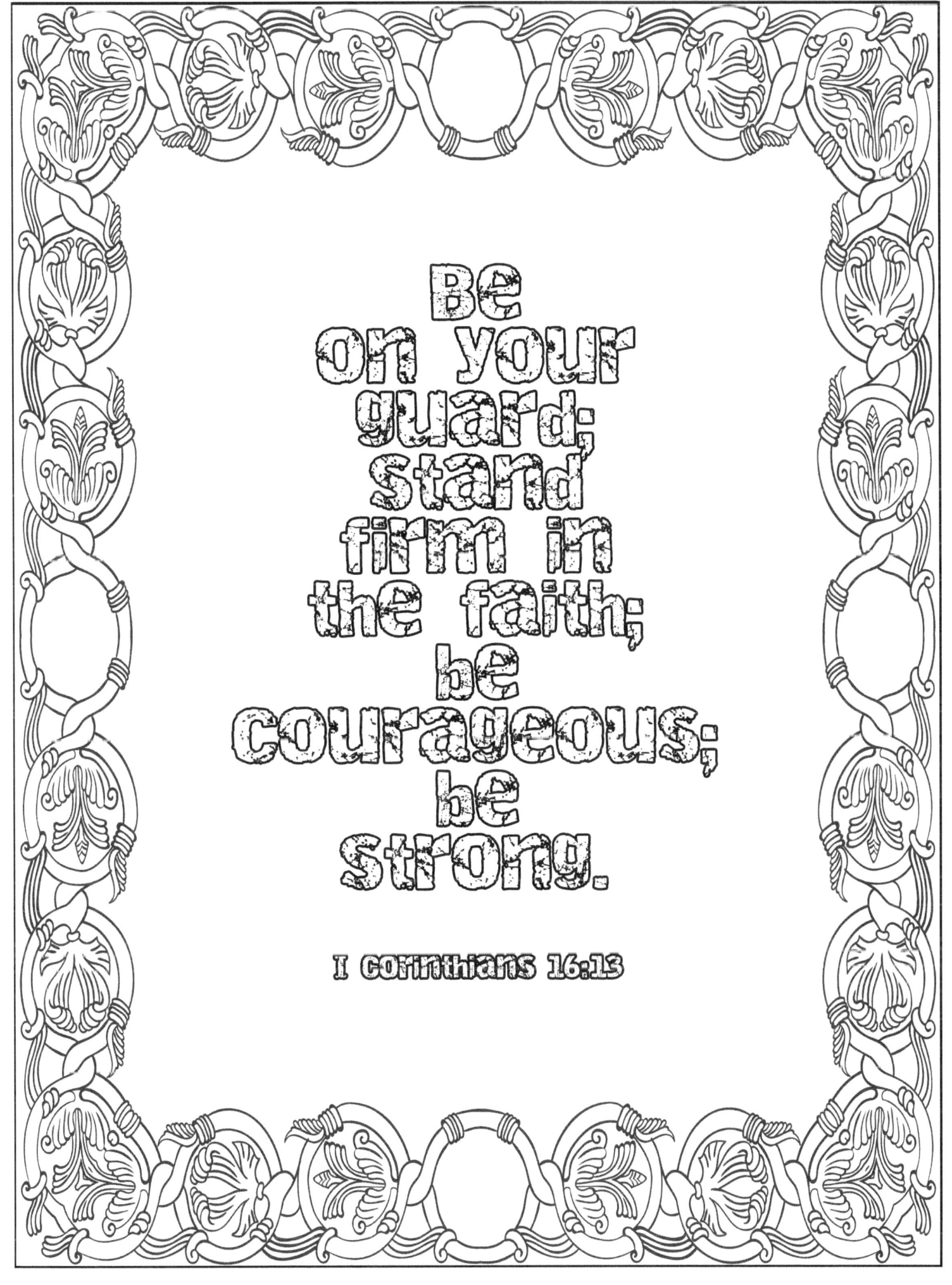

Be on your guard; stand firm in the faith; be courageous; be strong.

I Corinthians 16:13

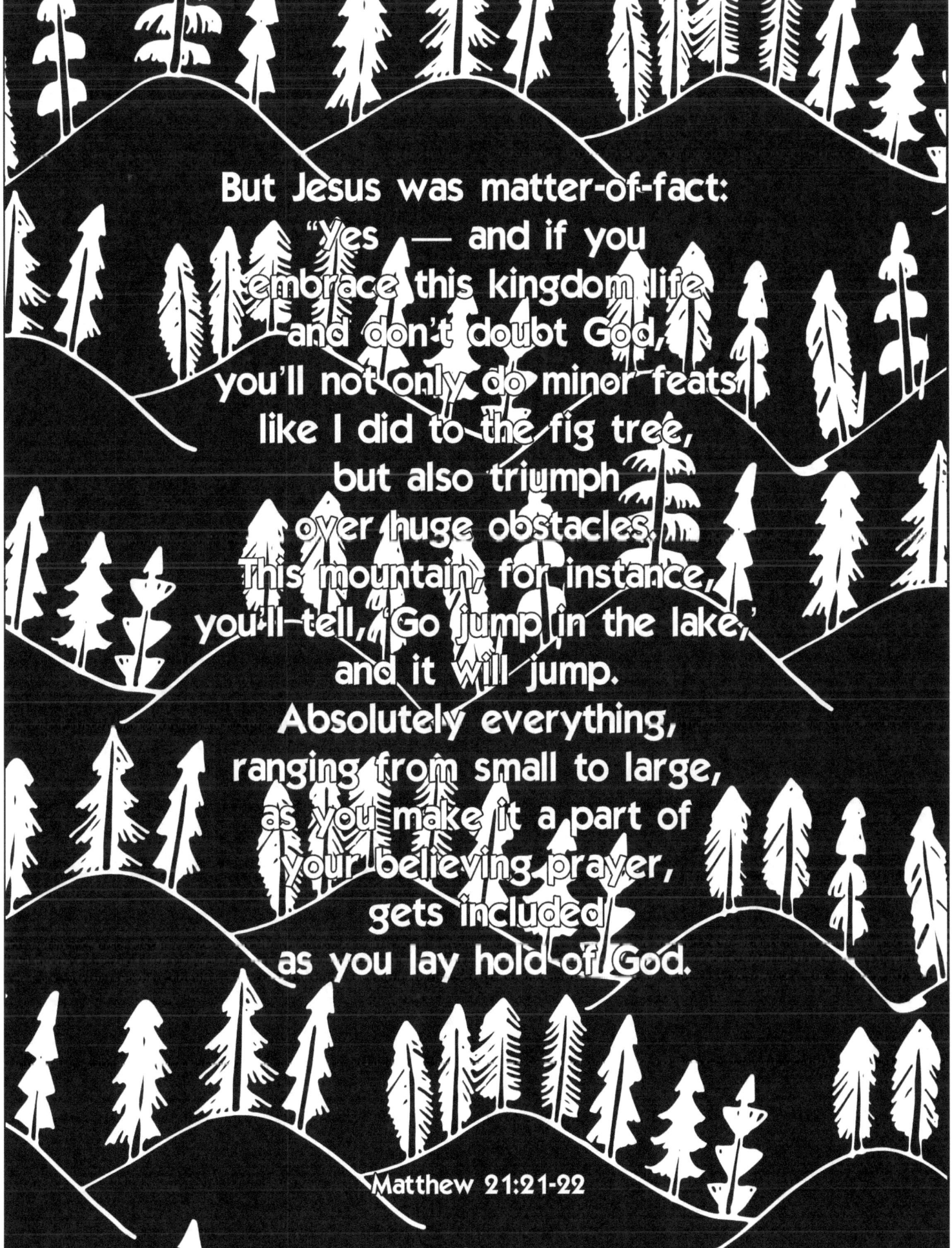

But Jesus was matter-of-fact:
"Yes — and if you
embrace this kingdom life
and don't doubt God,
you'll not only do minor feats
like I did to the fig tree,
but also triumph
over huge obstacles.
This mountain, for instance,
you'll tell, 'Go jump in the lake,'
and it will jump.
Absolutely everything,
ranging from small to large,
as you make it a part of
your believing prayer,
gets included
as you lay hold of God.

Matthew 21:21-22

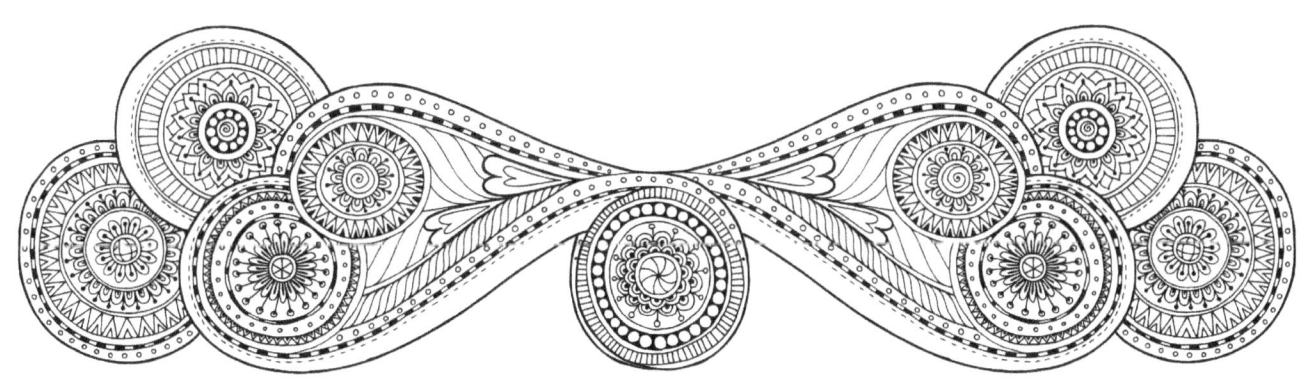

Pursue righteousness, godliness, faith, love patience, gentleness.

1 Timothy 6:11

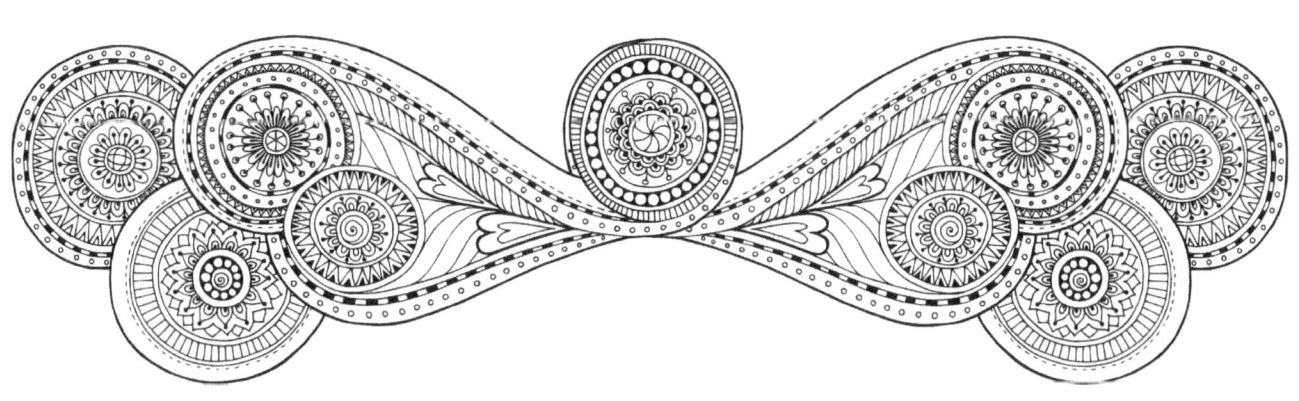

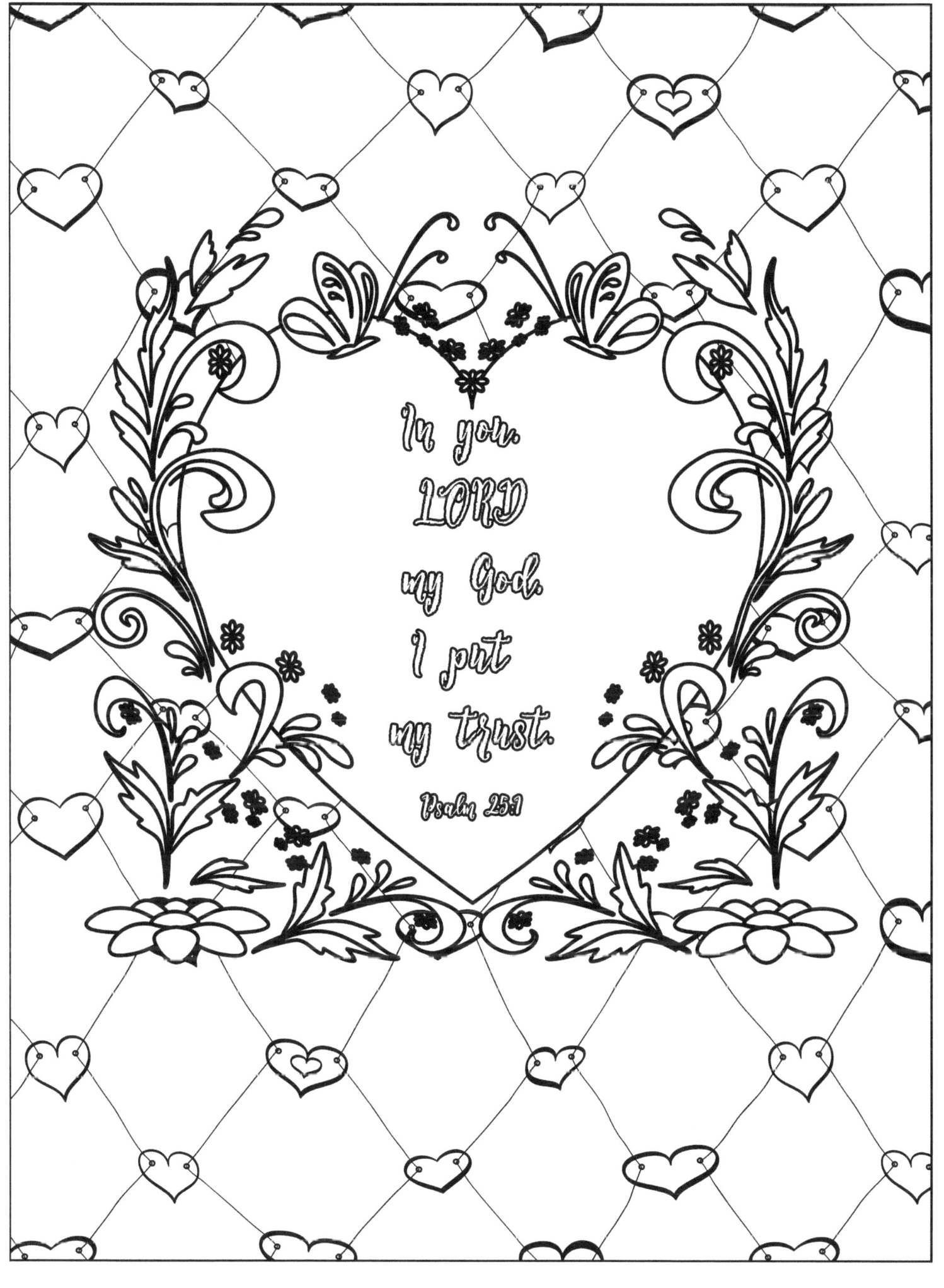

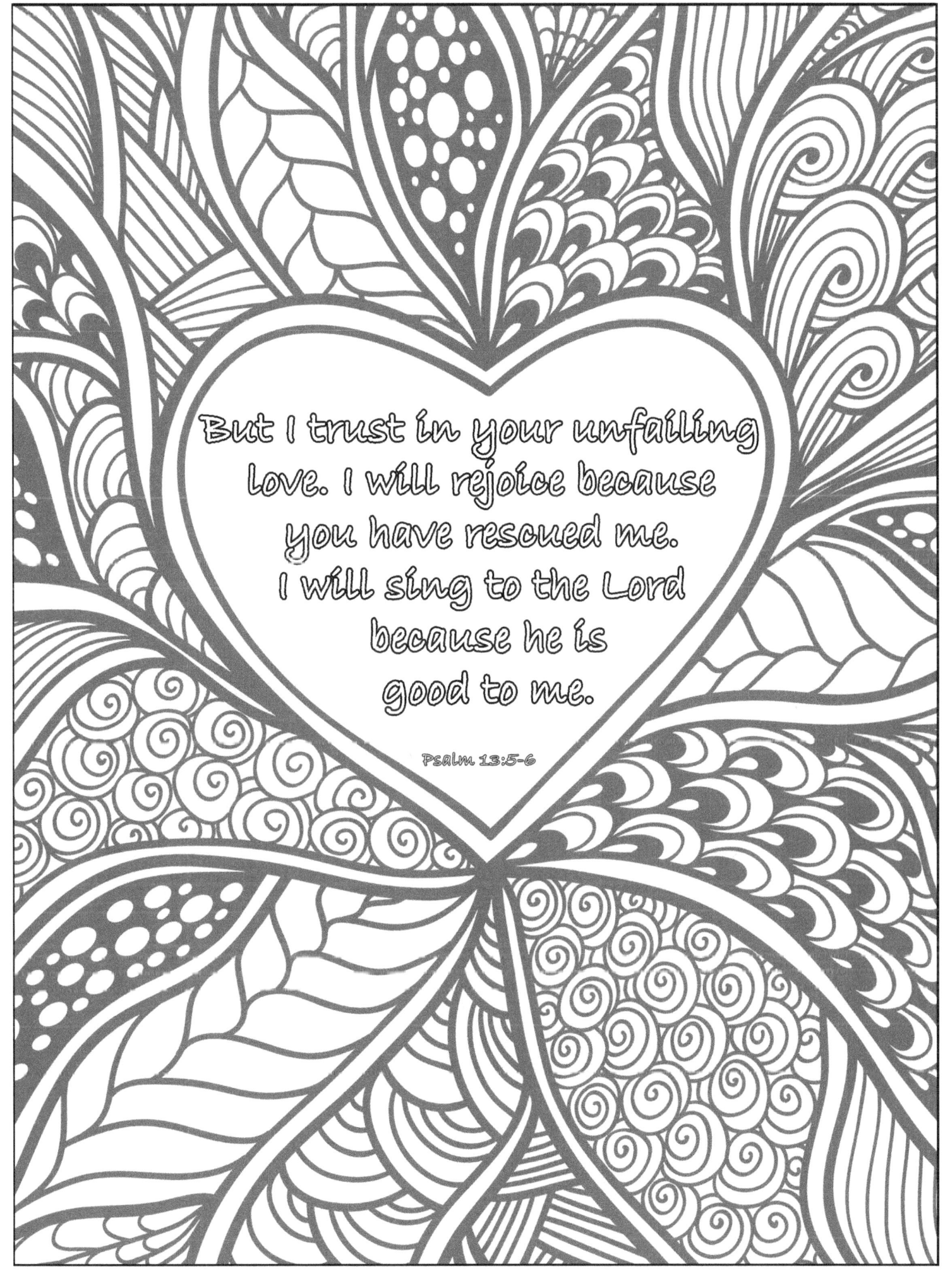

But I trust in your unfailing love. I will rejoice because you have rescued me. I will sing to the Lord because he is good to me.

Psalm 13:5-6

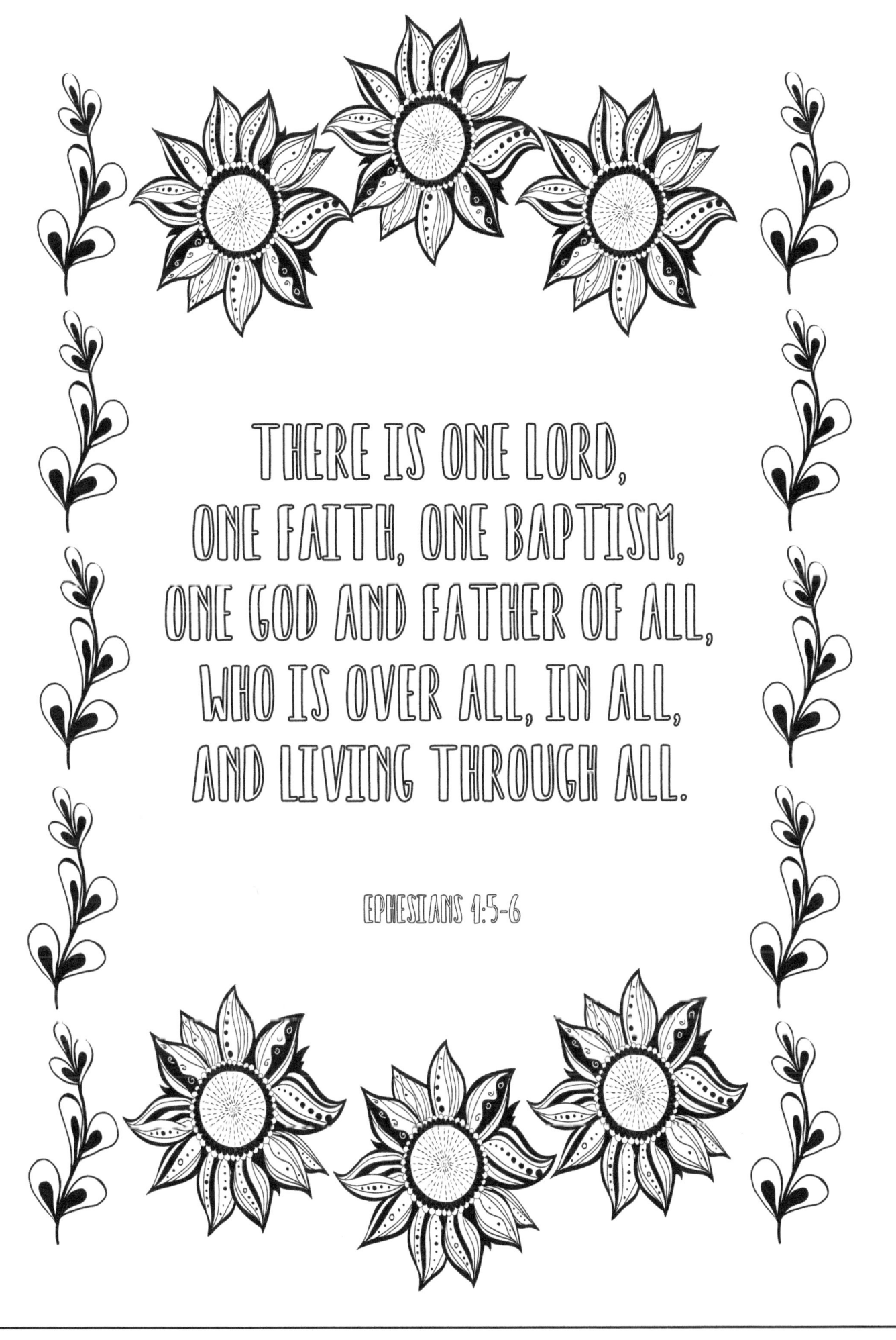

THERE IS ONE LORD,
ONE FAITH, ONE BAPTISM,
ONE GOD AND FATHER OF ALL,
WHO IS OVER ALL, IN ALL,
AND LIVING THROUGH ALL.

EPHESIANS 4:5-6

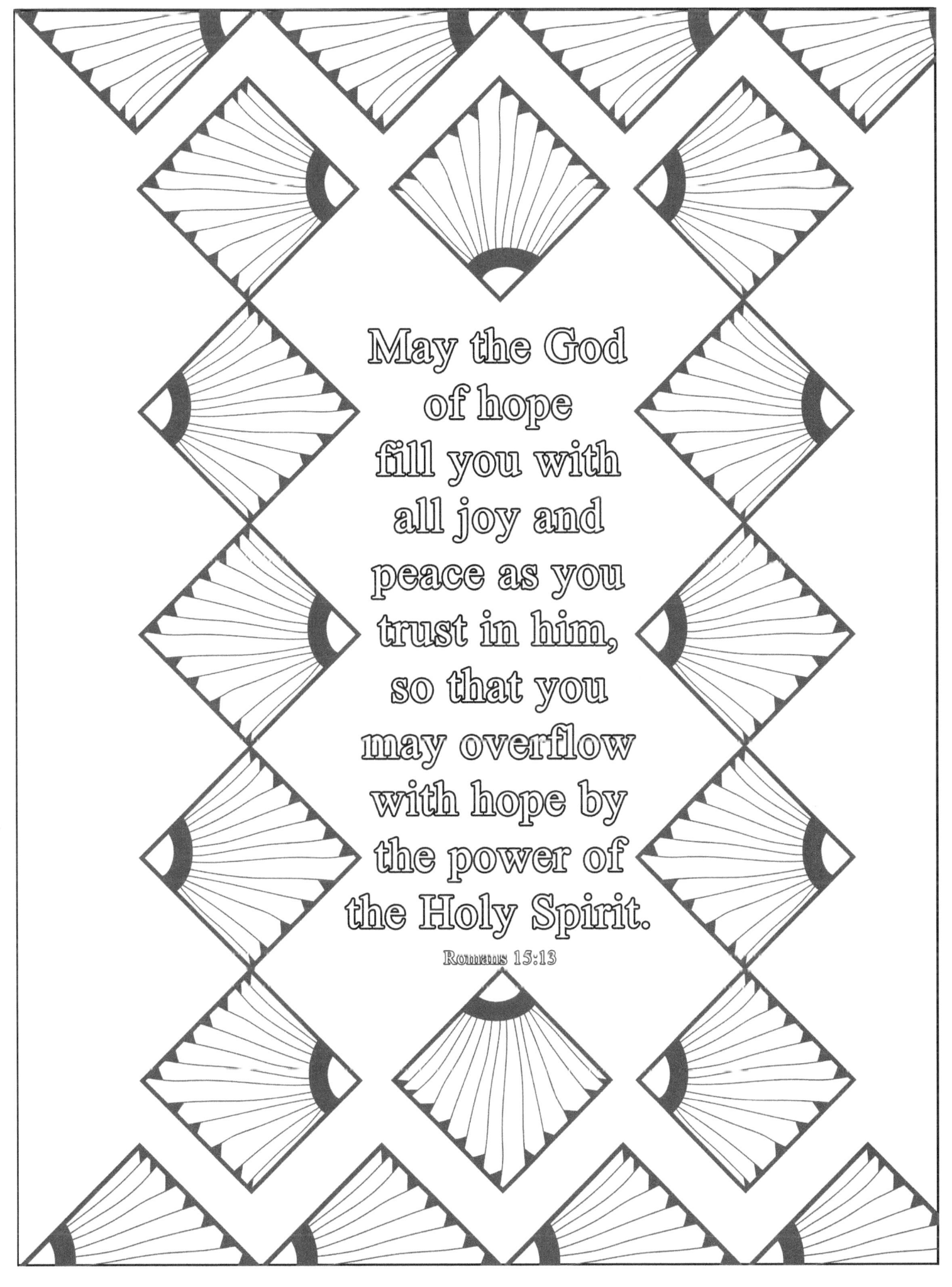

May the God
of hope
fill you with
all joy and
peace as you
trust in him,
so that you
may overflow
with hope by
the power of
the Holy Spirit.

Romans 15:13

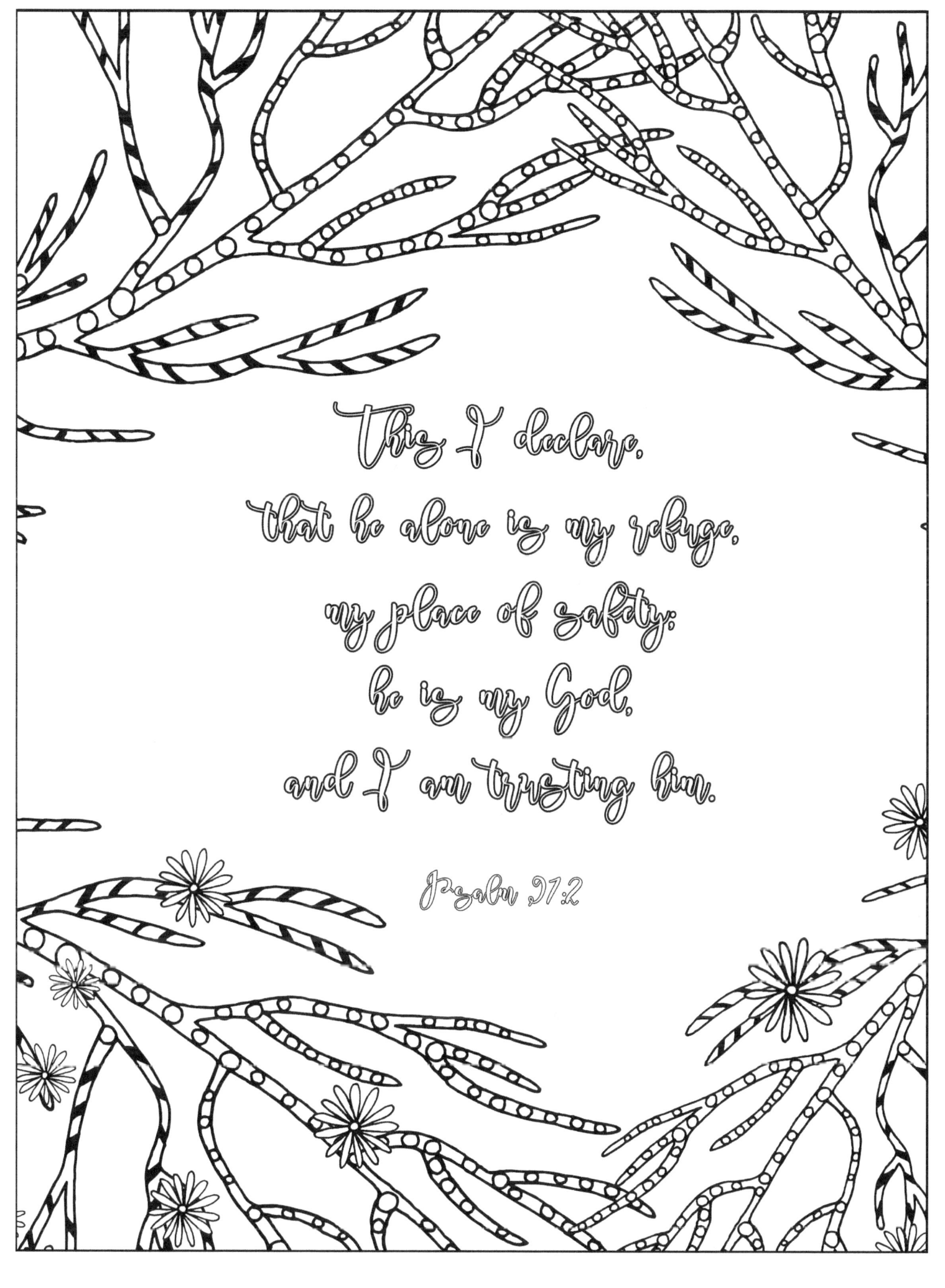

This I declare,
that he alone is my refuge,
my place of safety;
he is my God,
and I am trusting him.

Psalm 91:2

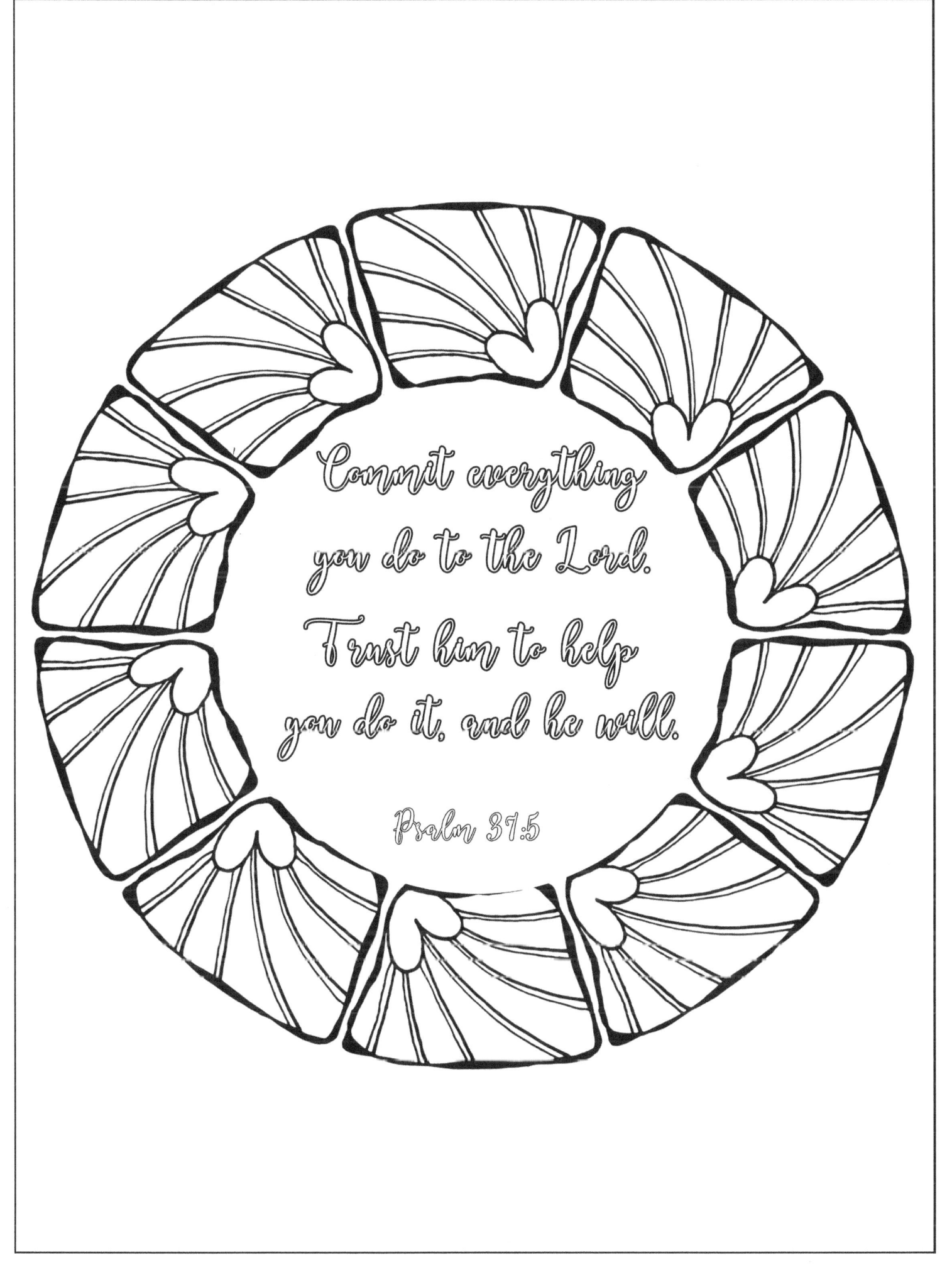

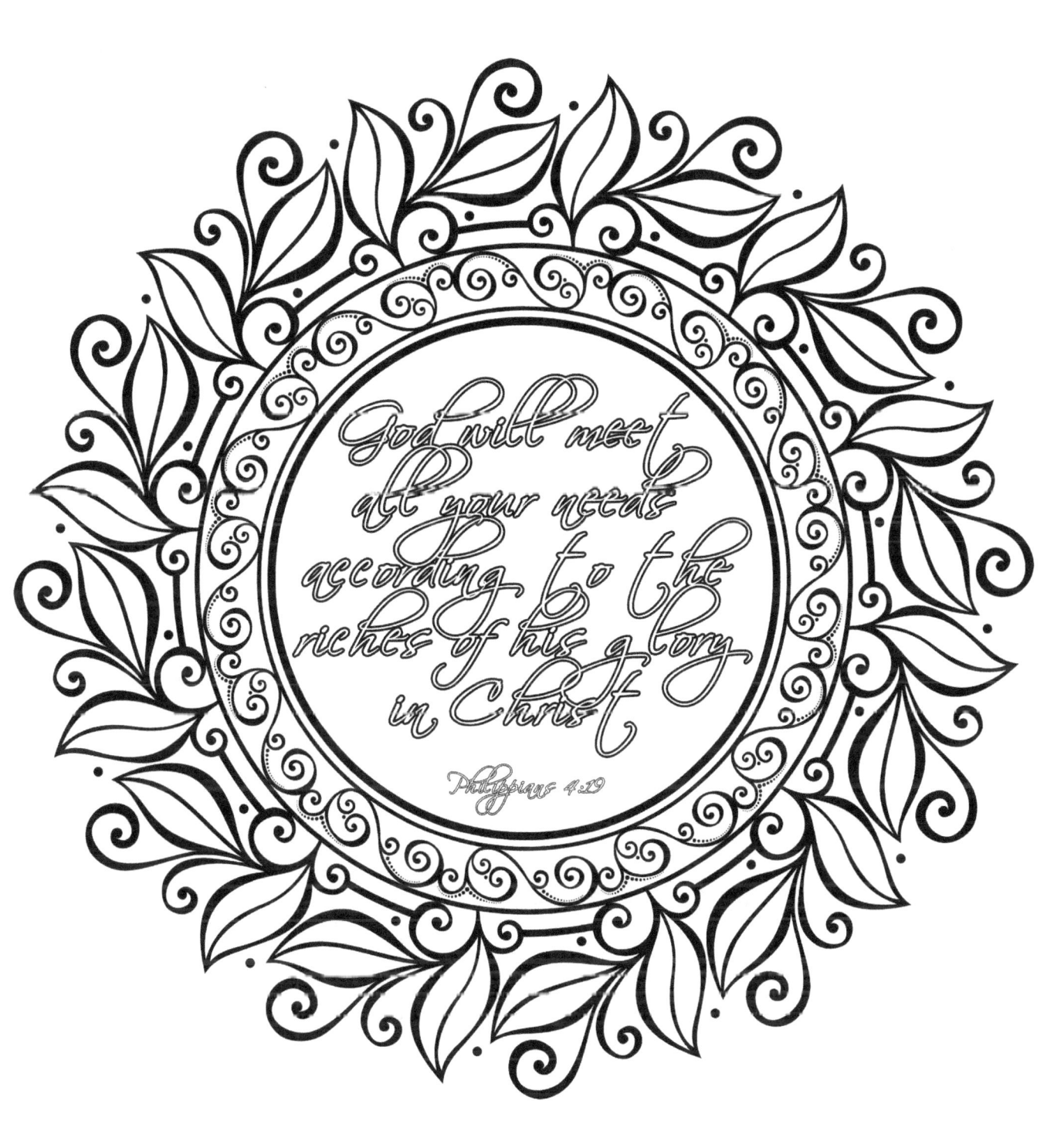

God will meet
all your needs
according to the
riches of his glory
in Christ

Philippians 4:19

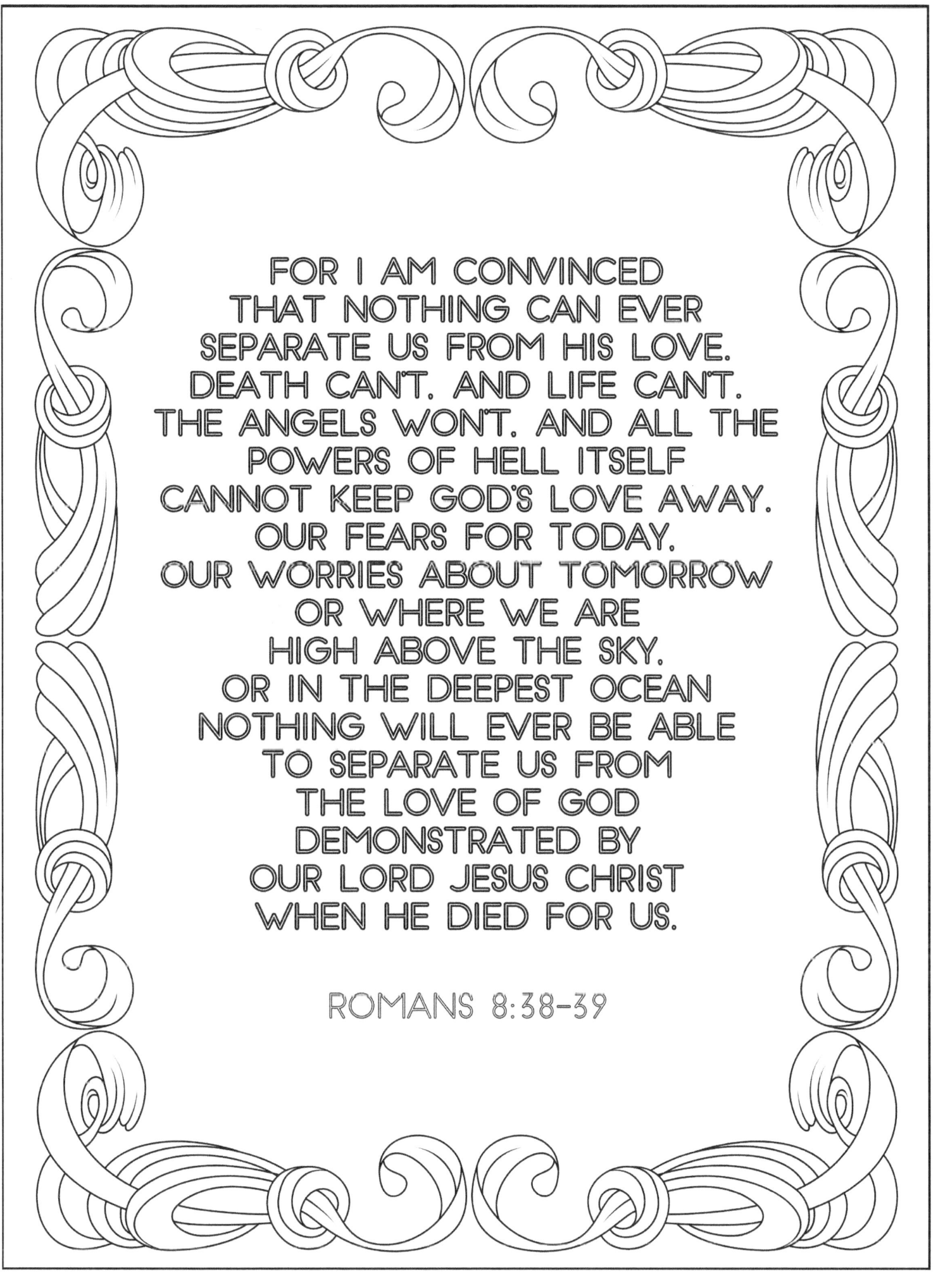

FOR I AM CONVINCED
THAT NOTHING CAN EVER
SEPARATE US FROM HIS LOVE.
DEATH CAN'T. AND LIFE CAN'T.
THE ANGELS WON'T. AND ALL THE
POWERS OF HELL ITSELF
CANNOT KEEP GOD'S LOVE AWAY.
OUR FEARS FOR TODAY.
OUR WORRIES ABOUT TOMORROW
OR WHERE WE ARE
HIGH ABOVE THE SKY.
OR IN THE DEEPEST OCEAN
NOTHING WILL EVER BE ABLE
TO SEPARATE US FROM
THE LOVE OF GOD
DEMONSTRATED BY
OUR LORD JESUS CHRIST
WHEN HE DIED FOR US.

ROMANS 8:38-39

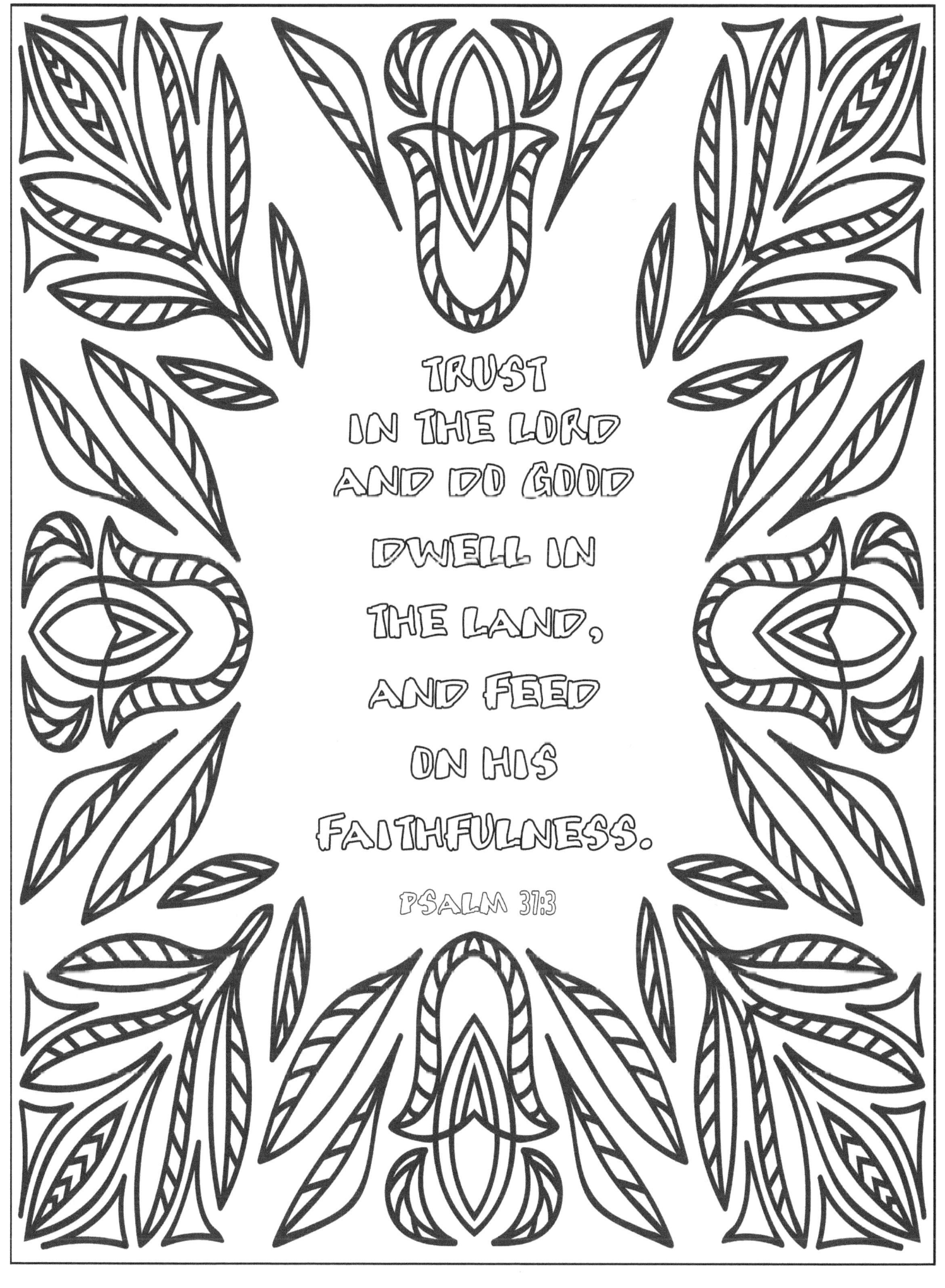

TRUST IN THE LORD AND DO GOOD DWELL IN THE LAND, AND FEED ON HIS FAITHFULNESS.

PSALM 37:3

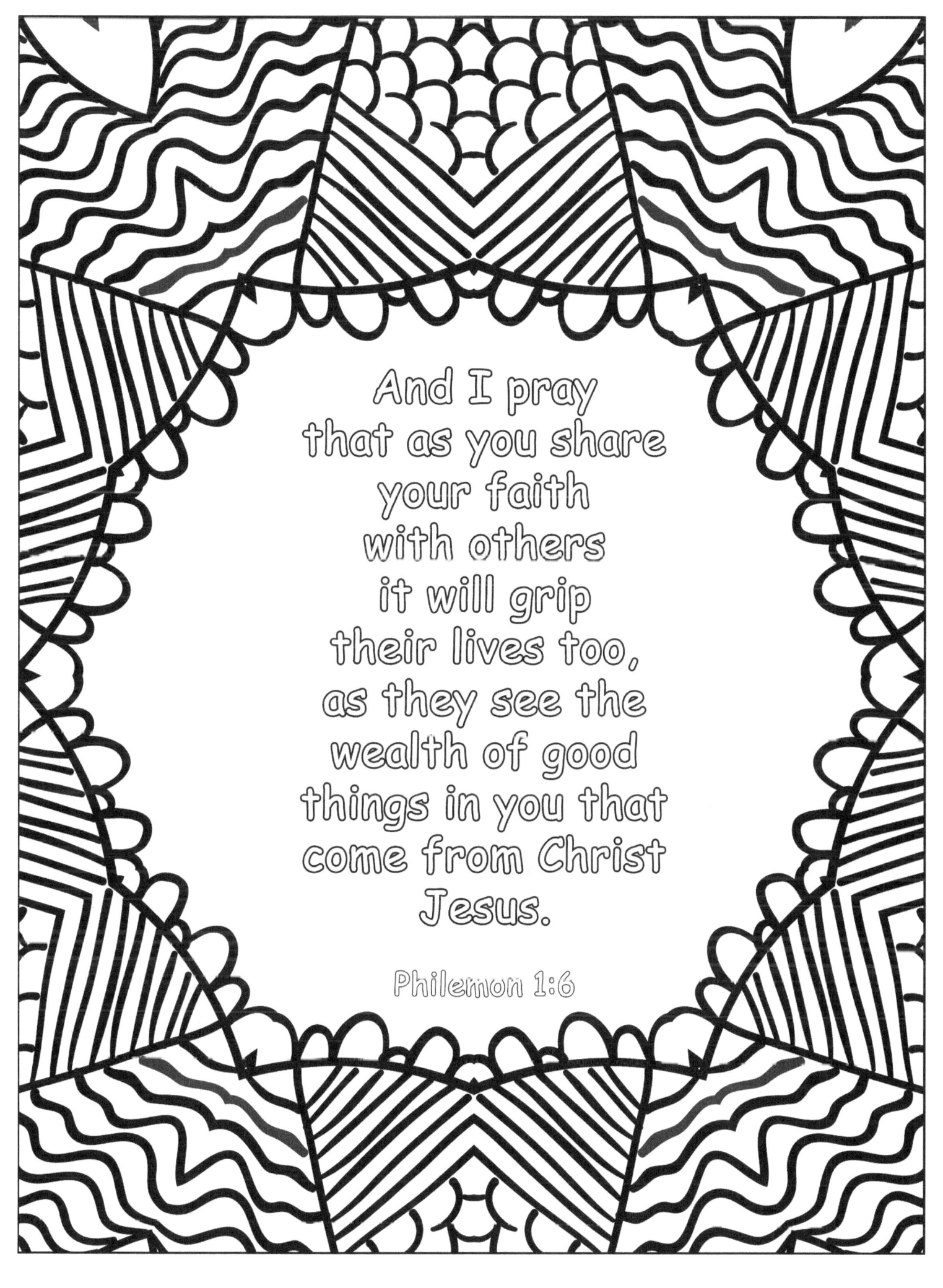

And I pray
that as you share
your faith
with others
it will grip
their lives too,
as they see the
wealth of good
things in you that
come from Christ
Jesus.

Philemon 1:6

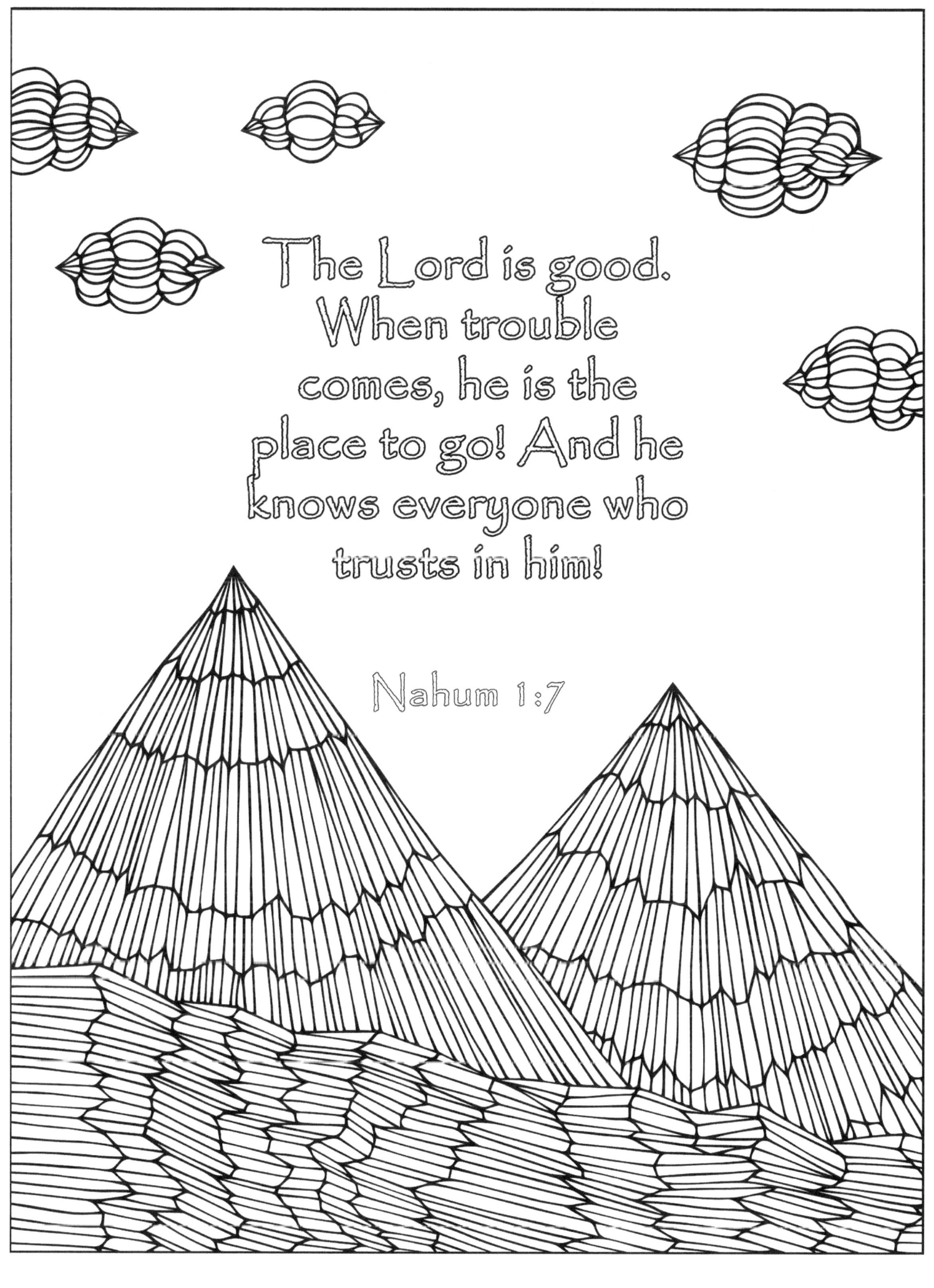

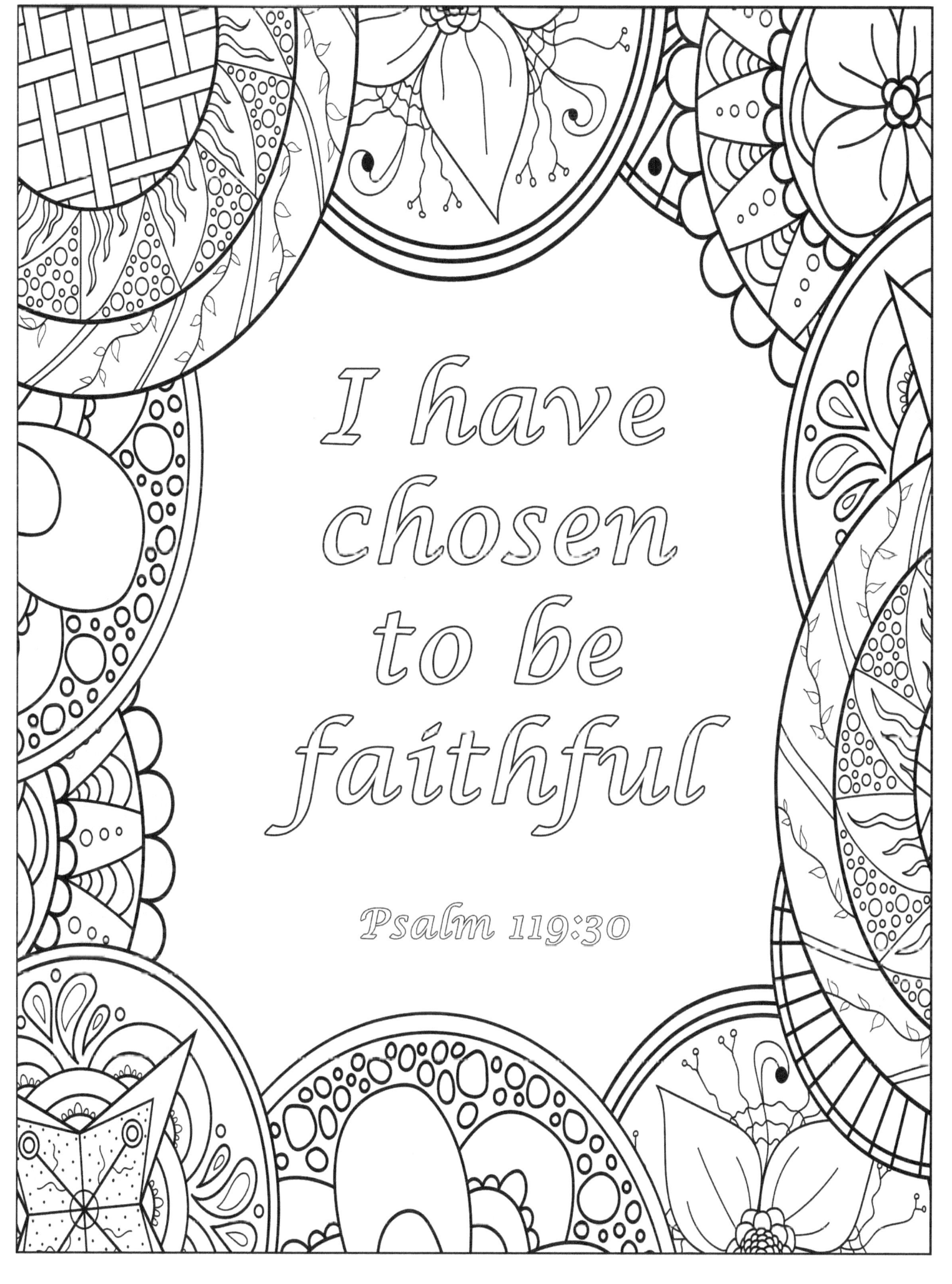

I have chosen to be faithful

Psalm 119:30

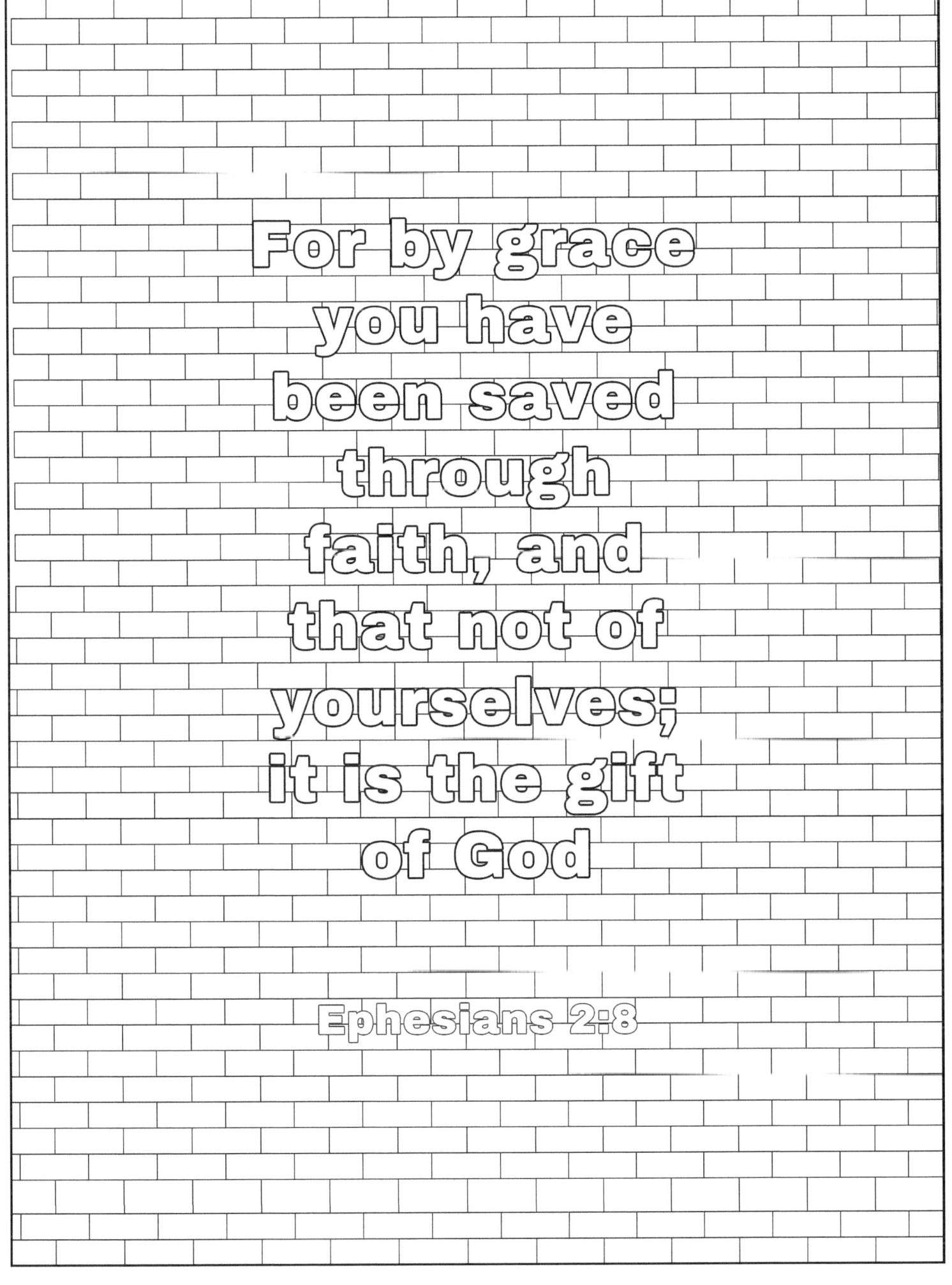

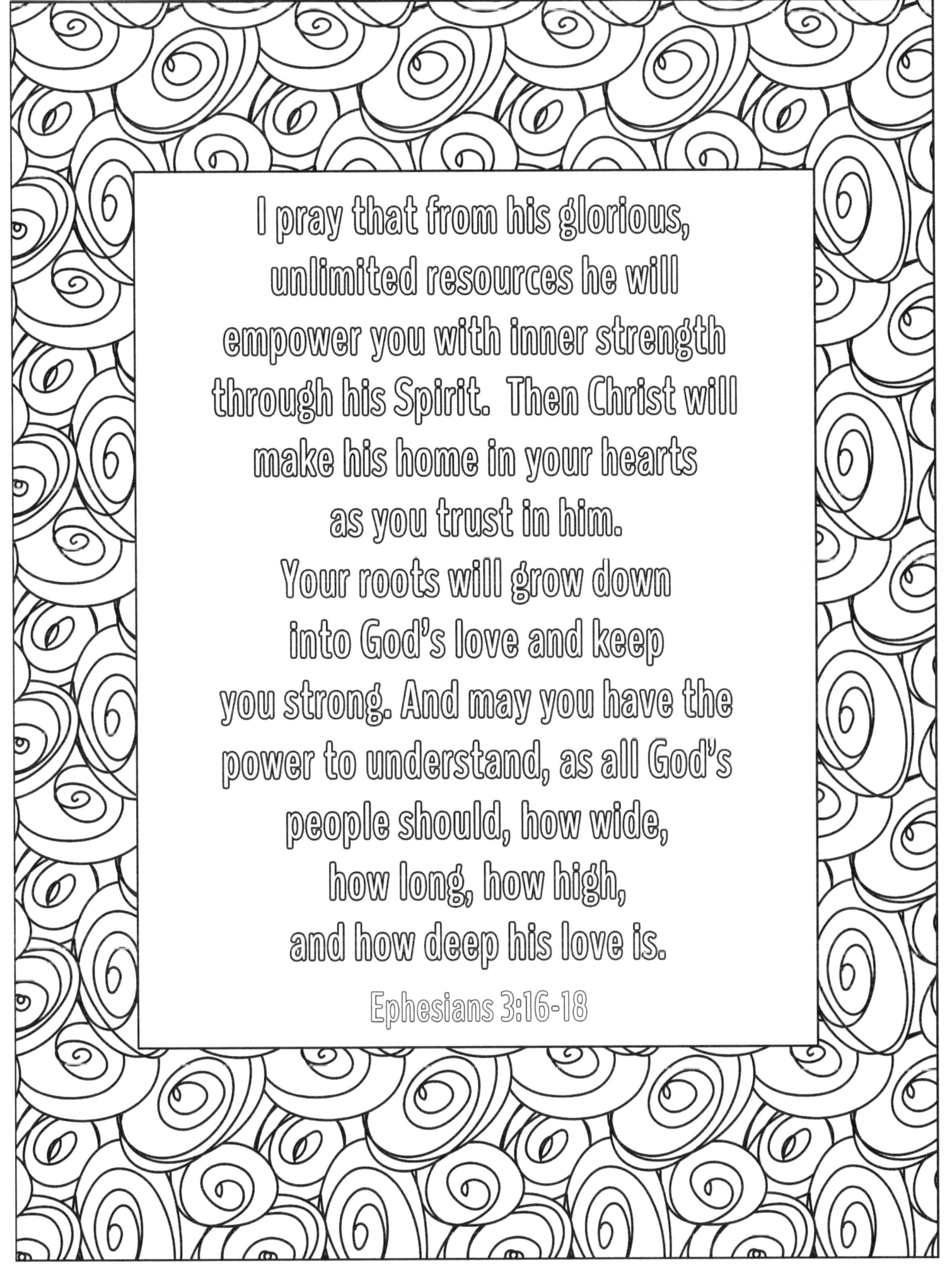

I pray that from his glorious,
unlimited resources he will
empower you with inner strength
through his Spirit. Then Christ will
make his home in your hearts
as you trust in him.
Your roots will grow down
into God's love and keep
you strong. And may you have the
power to understand, as all God's
people should, how wide,
how long, how high,
and how deep his love is.

Ephesians 3:16-18

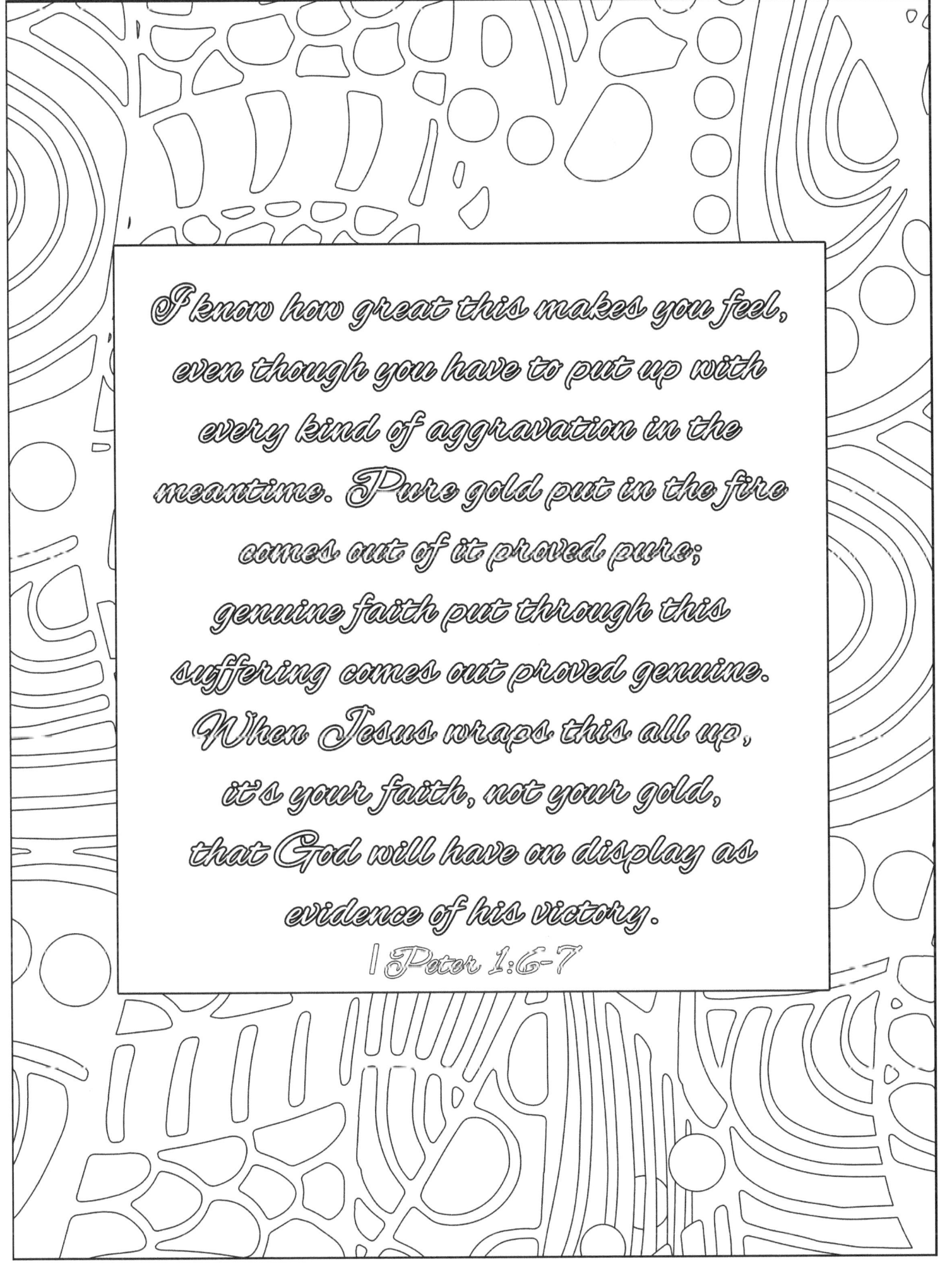

I know how great this makes you feel, even though you have to put up with every kind of aggravation in the meantime. Pure gold put in the fire comes out of it proved pure; genuine faith put through this suffering comes out proved genuine. When Jesus wraps this all up, it's your faith, not your gold, that God will have on display as evidence of his victory.

1 Peter 1:6-7

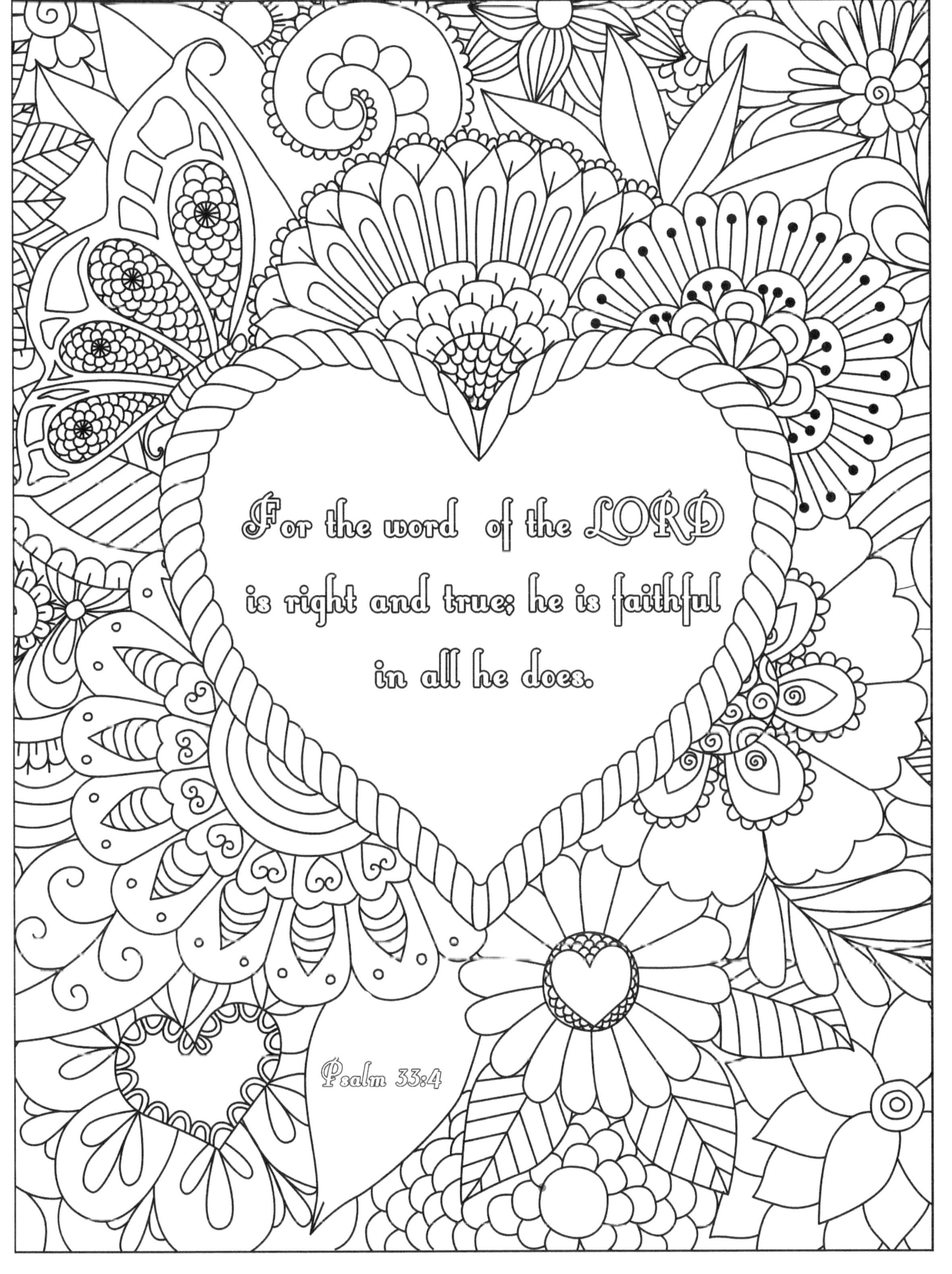

For the word of the LORD is right and true; he is faithful in all he does.

Psalm 33:4

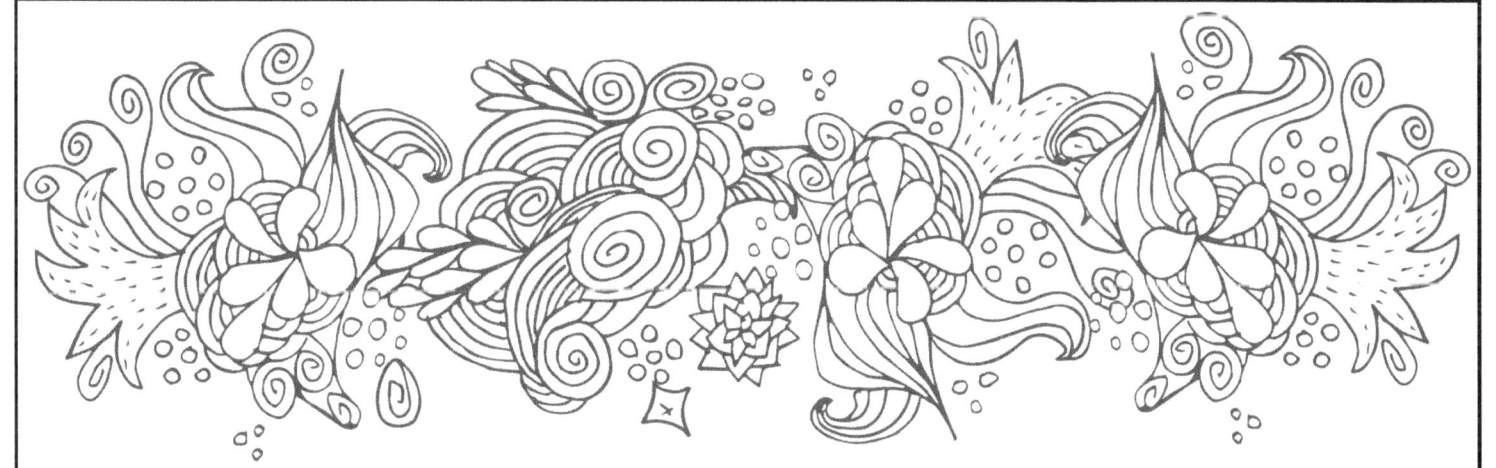

The Lord is my fort where I can
enter and be safe;
no one can follow me in and slay me.
He is a rugged mountain
where I hide; he is my Savior,
a rock where none can reach me,
and a tower of safety.
He is my shield. He is like the
strong horn of a mighty fighting bull.

Psalm 18:2

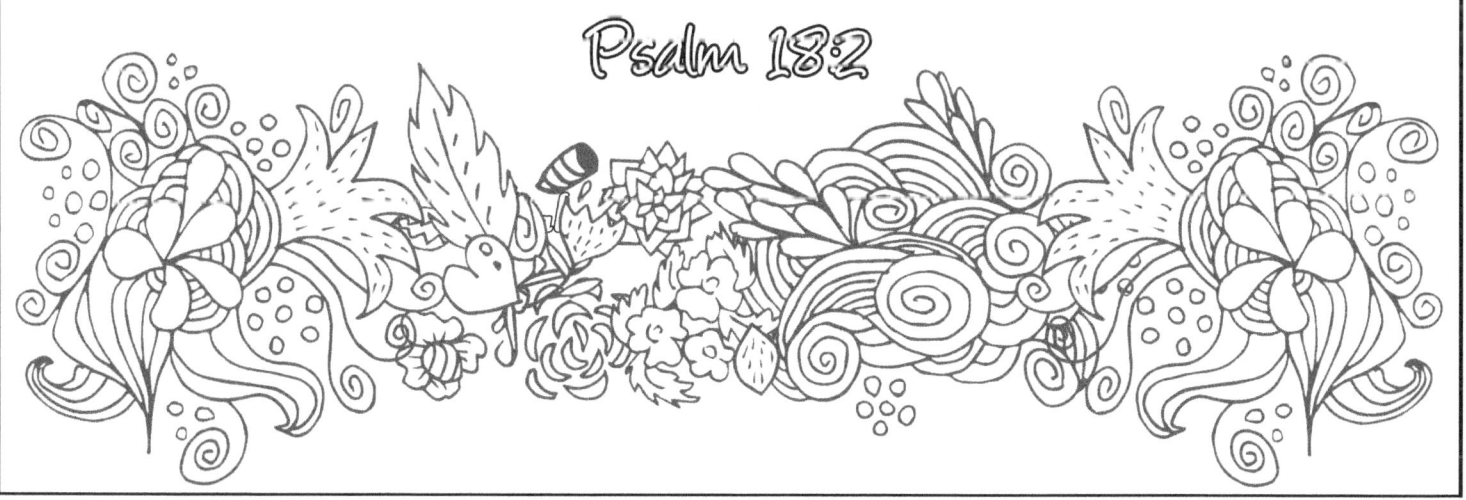

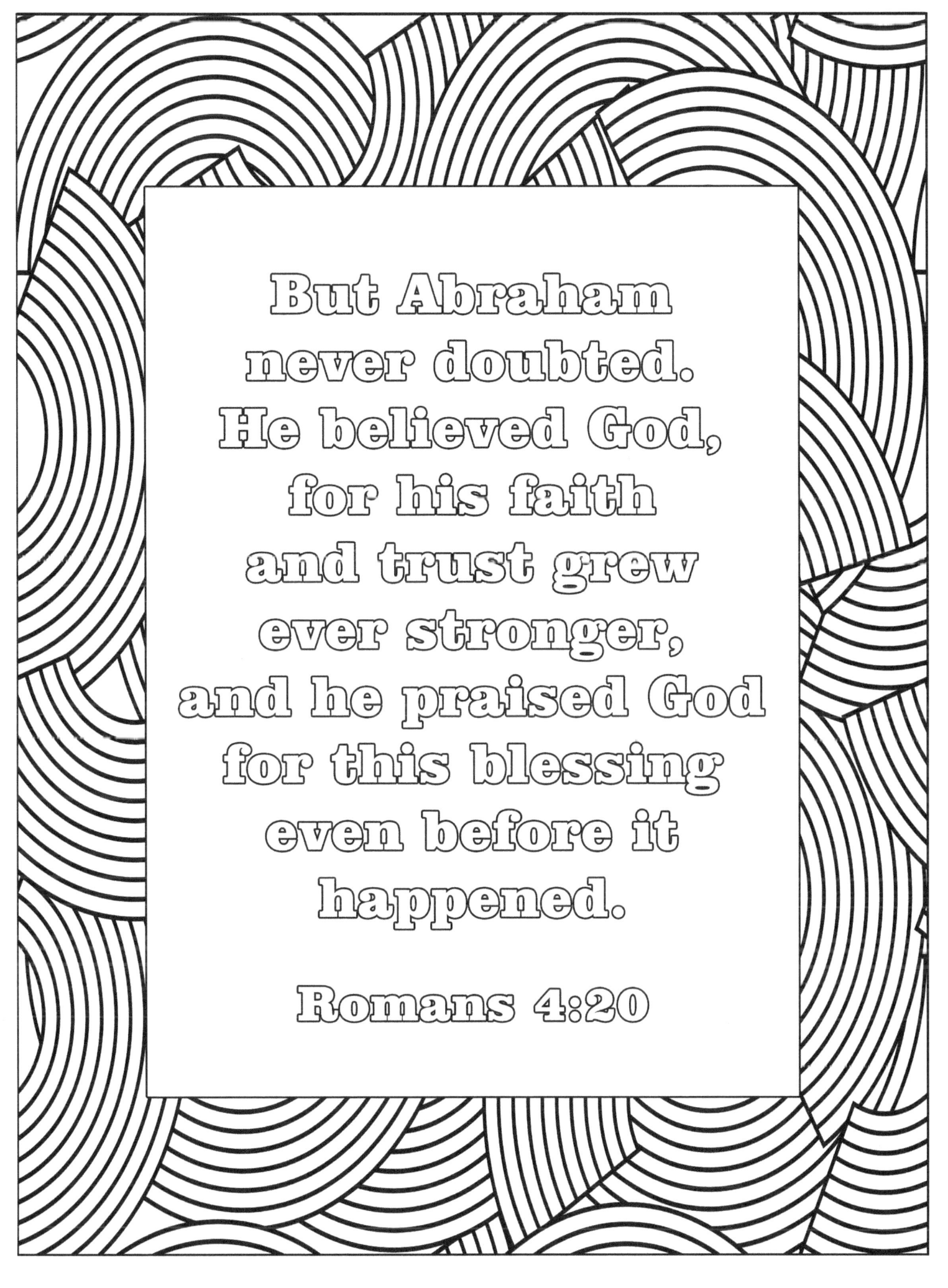

But Abraham never doubted. He believed God, for his faith and trust grew ever stronger, and he praised God for this blessing even before it happened.

Romans 4:20

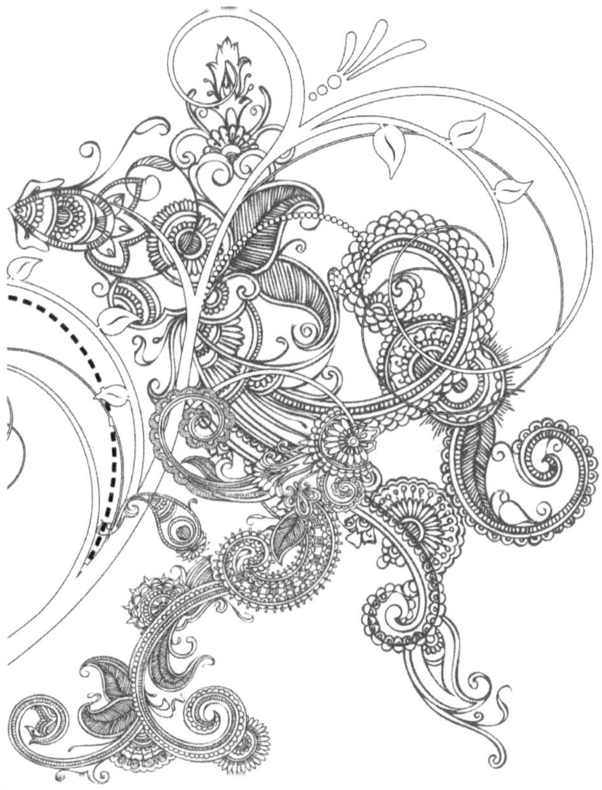

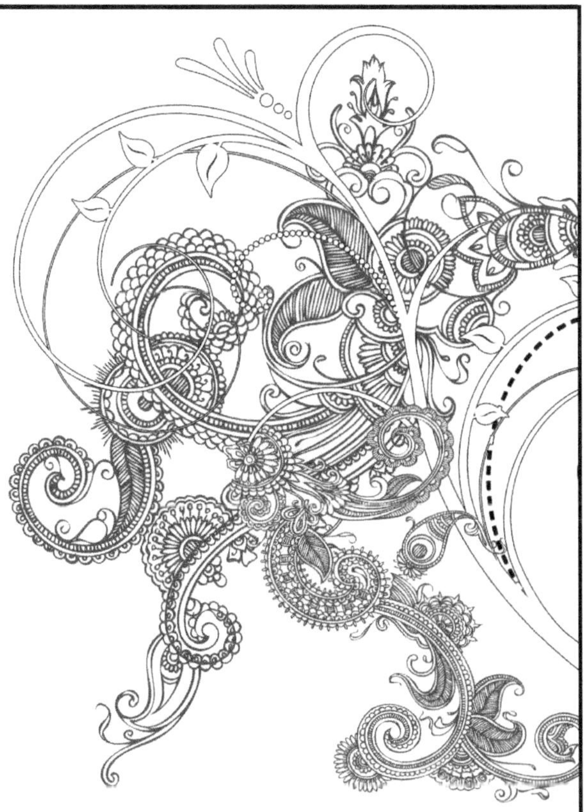

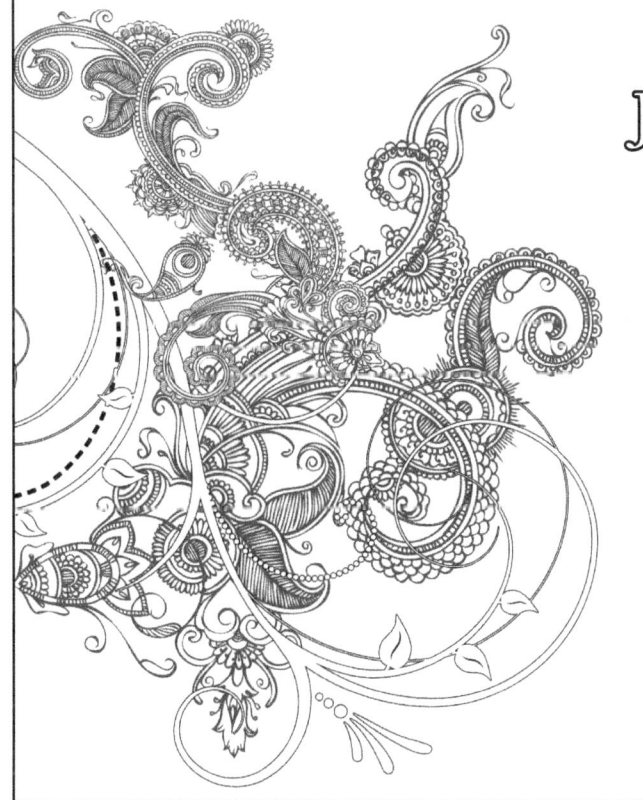
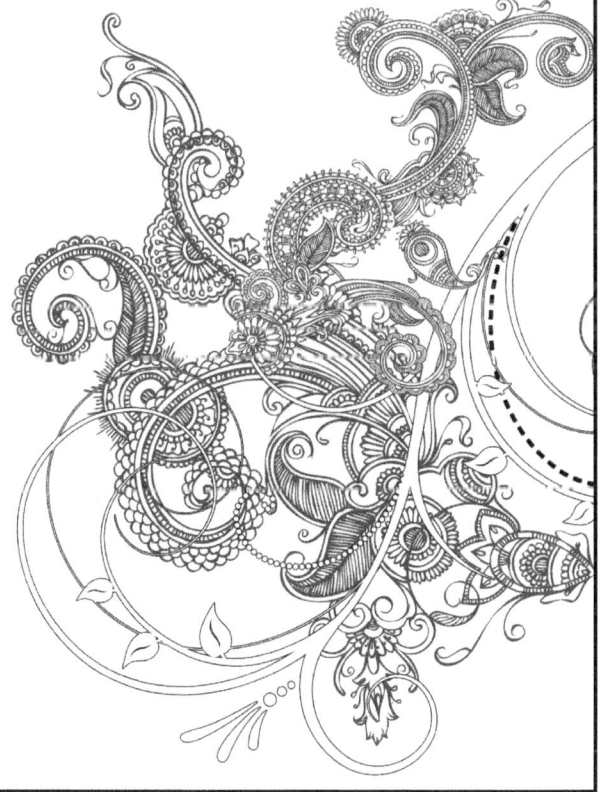

But when you ask, you must believe
and not doubt, because the one who
doubts is like a wave of the sea,
blown and tossed by the wind.

James 1:6

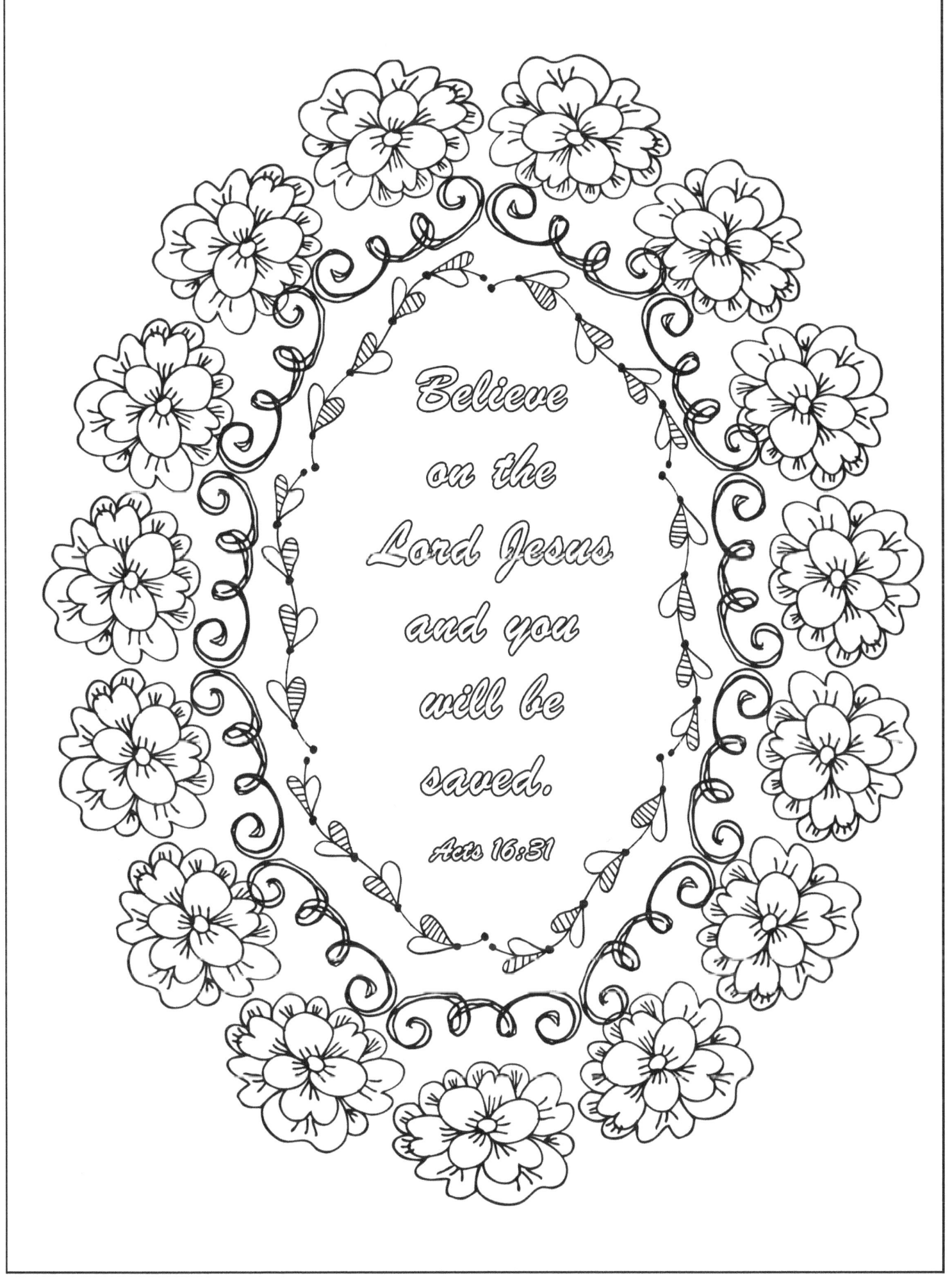

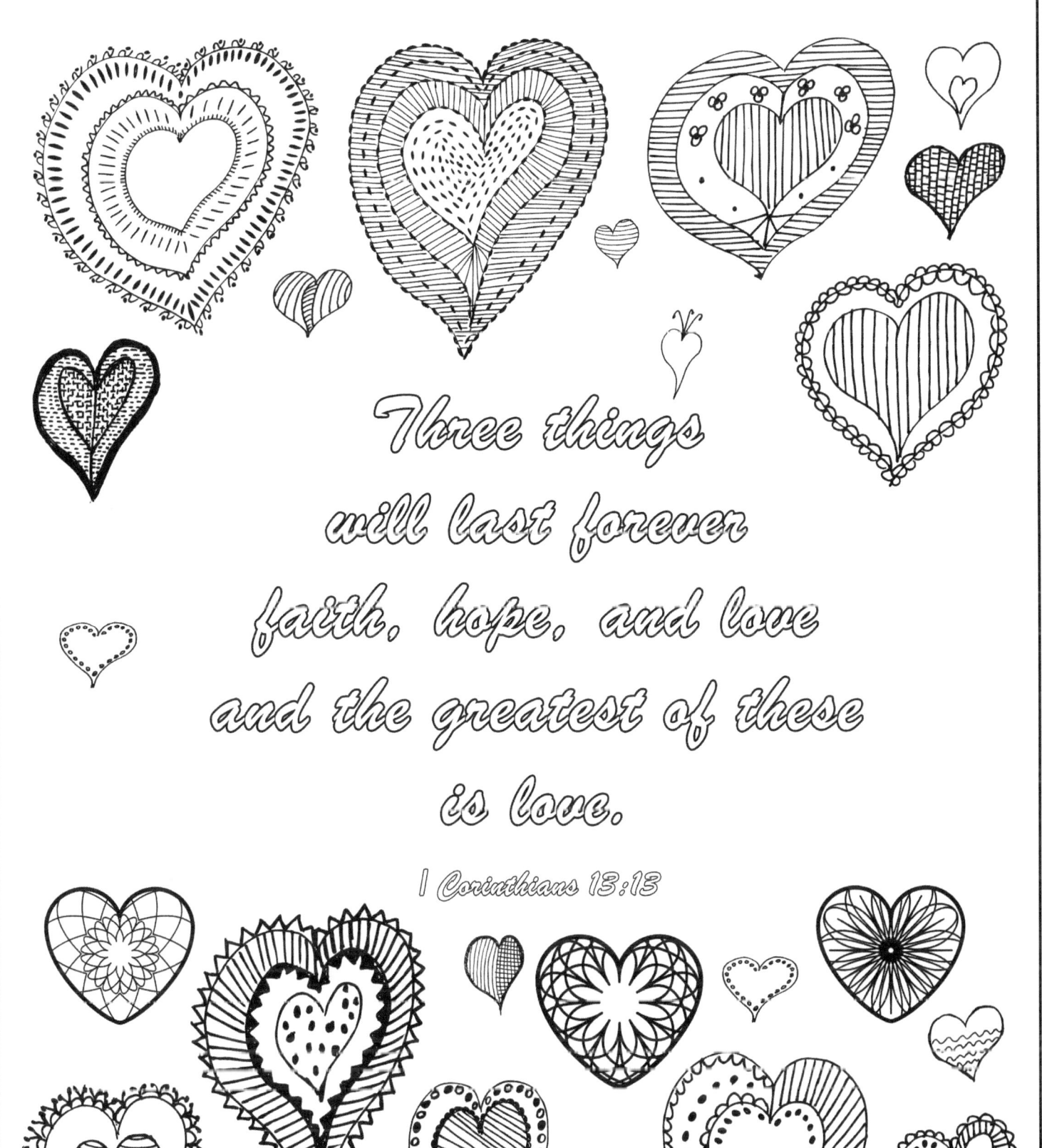

Three things
will last forever
faith, hope, and love
and the greatest of these
is love.

1 Corinthians 13:13

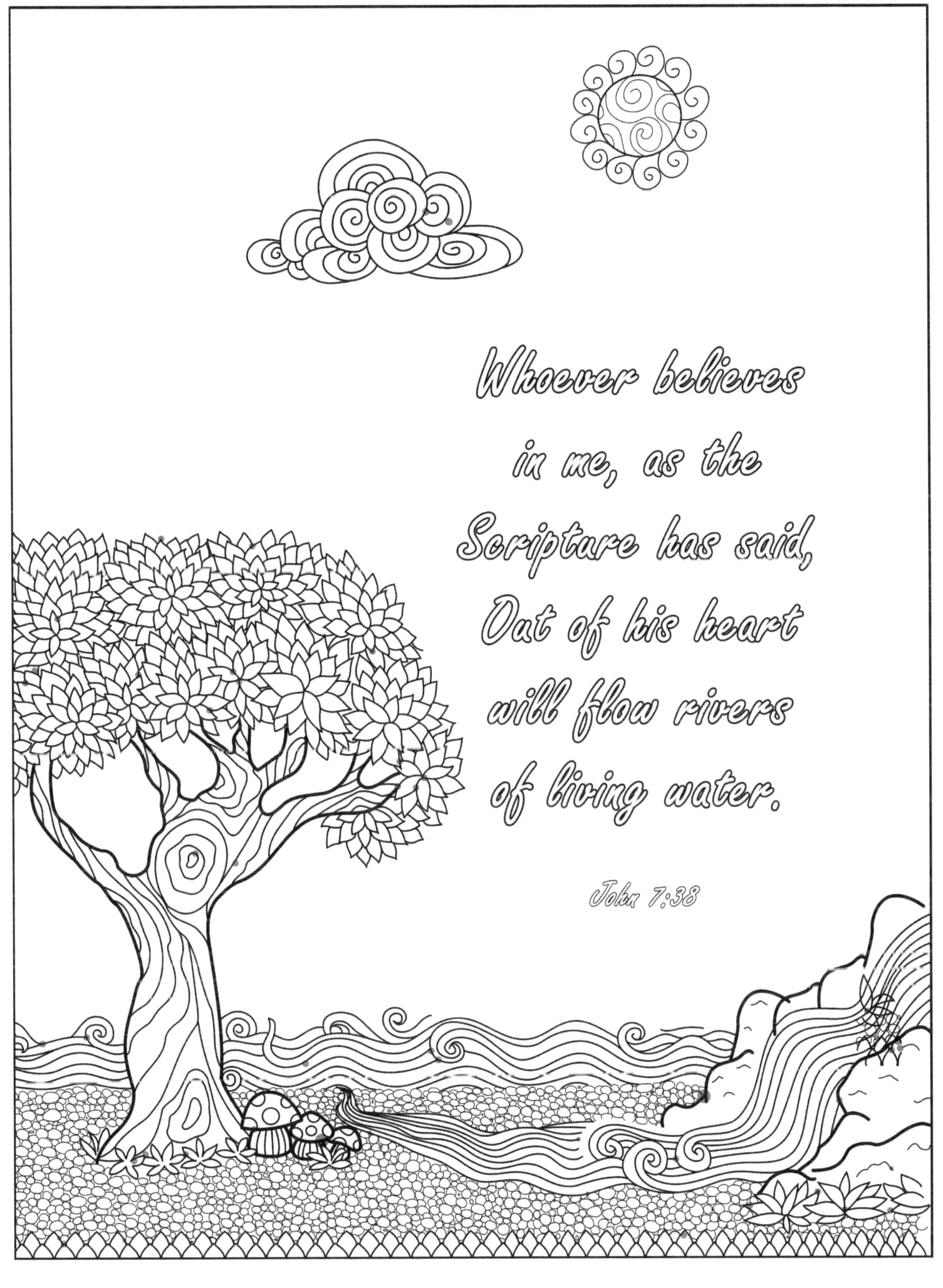

Whoever believes in me, as the Scripture has said, Out of his heart will flow rivers of living water.

John 7:38

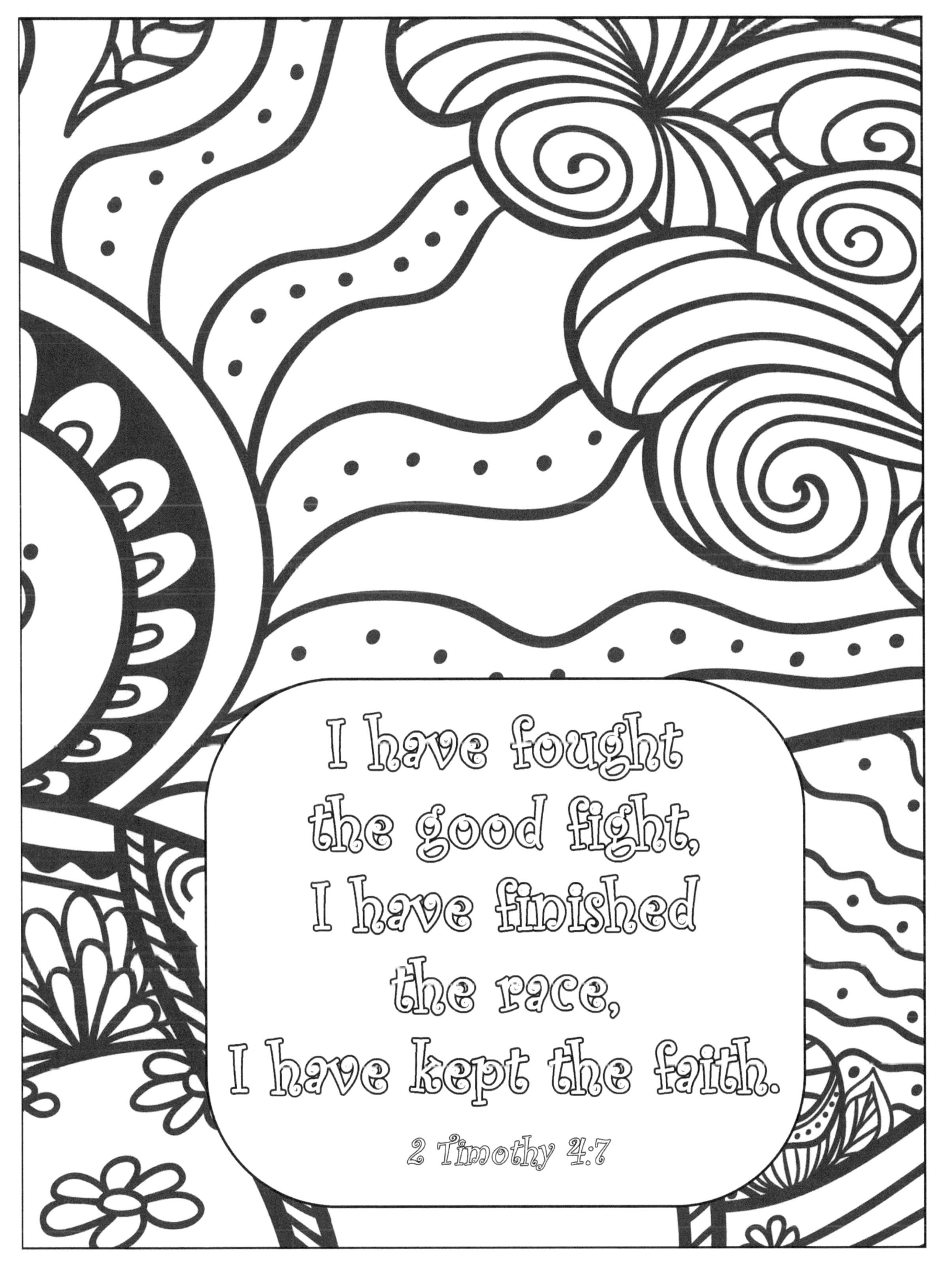

I have fought
the good fight,
I have finished
the race,
I have kept the faith.

2 Timothy 4:7

SO THEN FAITH COMES BY HEARING, AND HEARING BY THE WORD OF GOD.

ROMANS 10:17

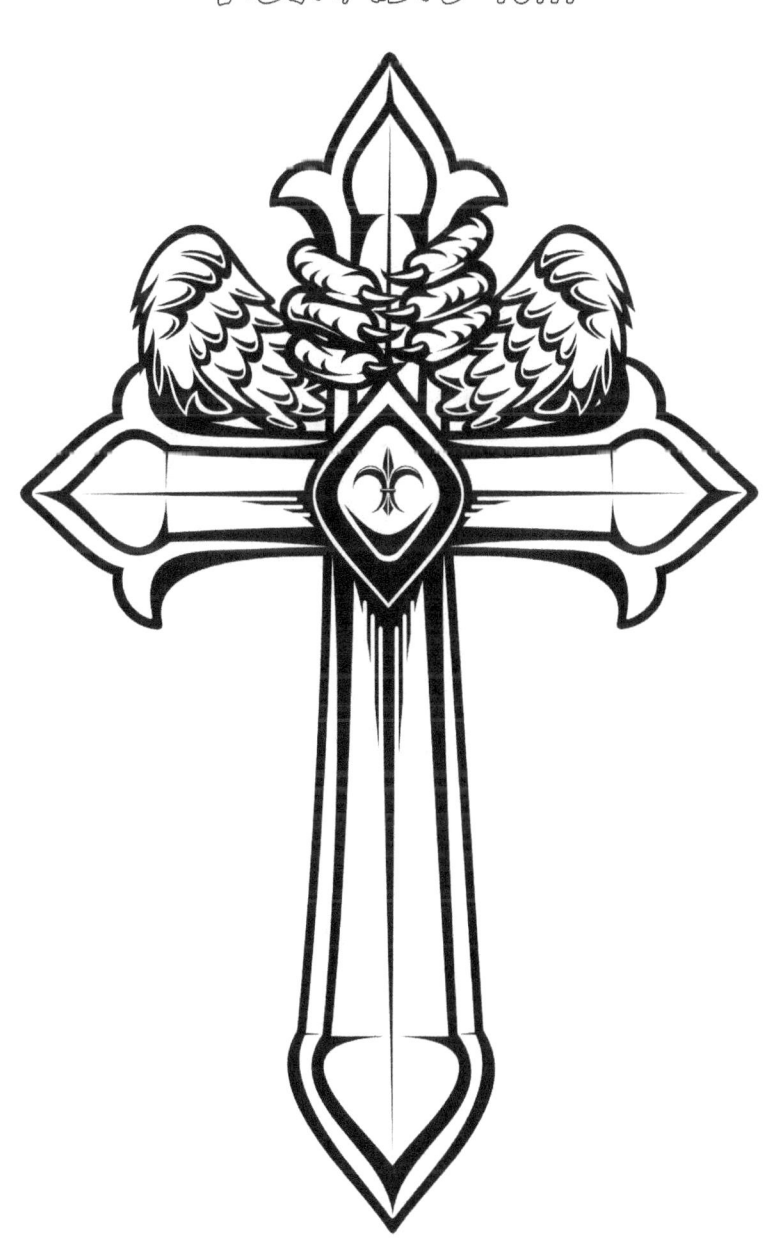

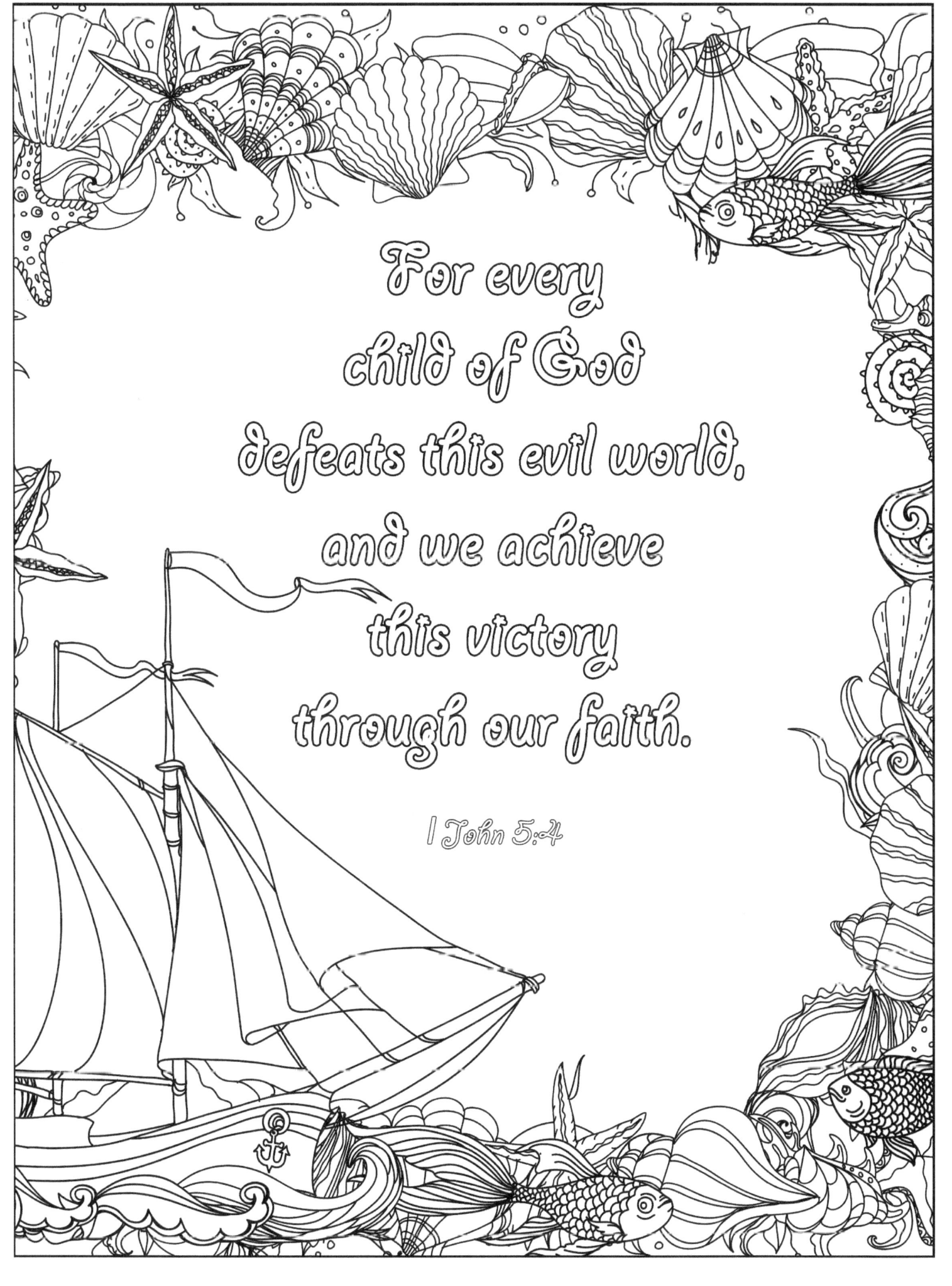

For every
child of God
defeats this evil world,
and we achieve
this victory
through our faith.

1 John 5:4

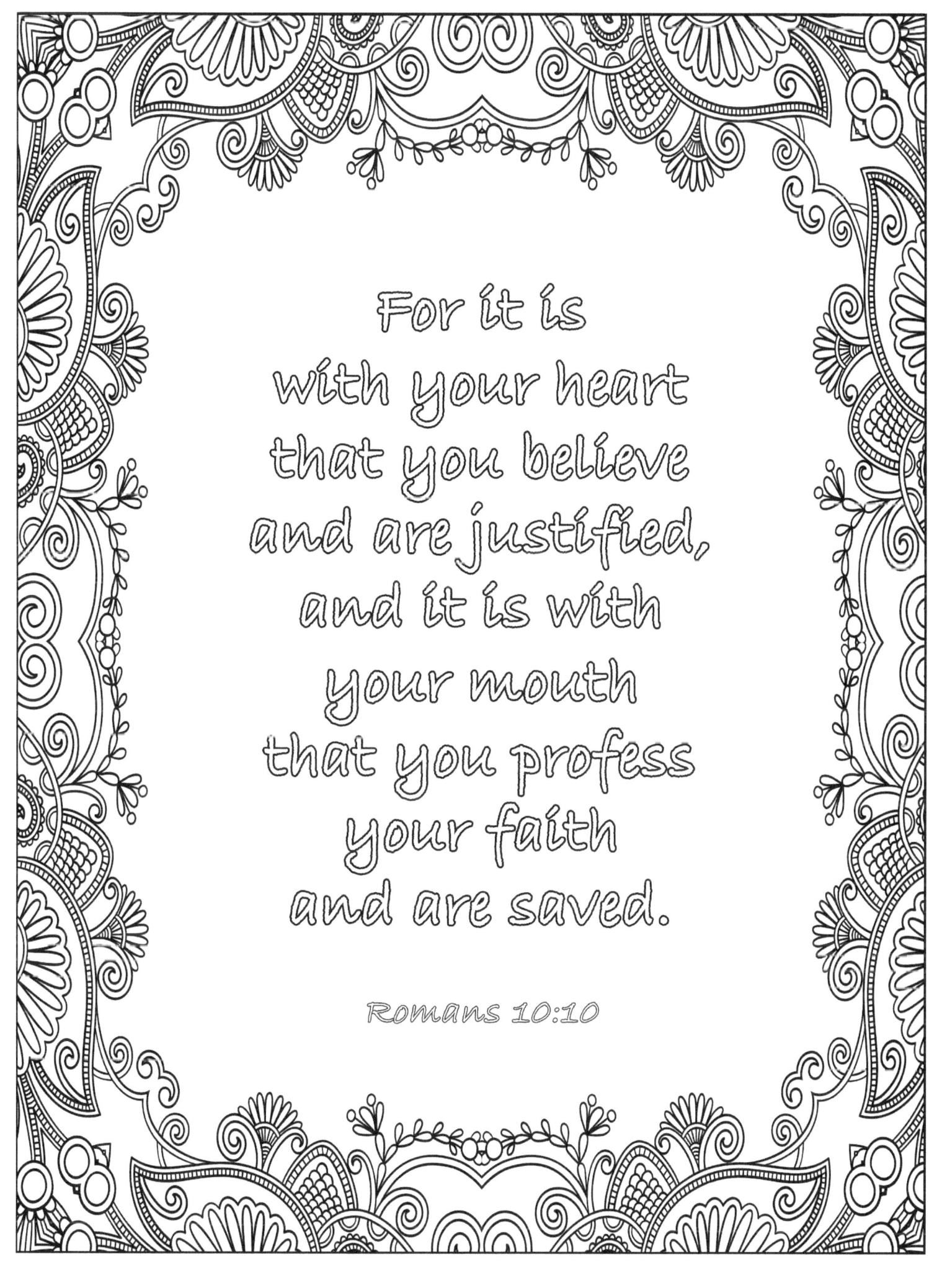

For it is
with your heart
that you believe
and are justified,
and it is with
your mouth
that you profess
your faith
and are saved.

Romans 10:10

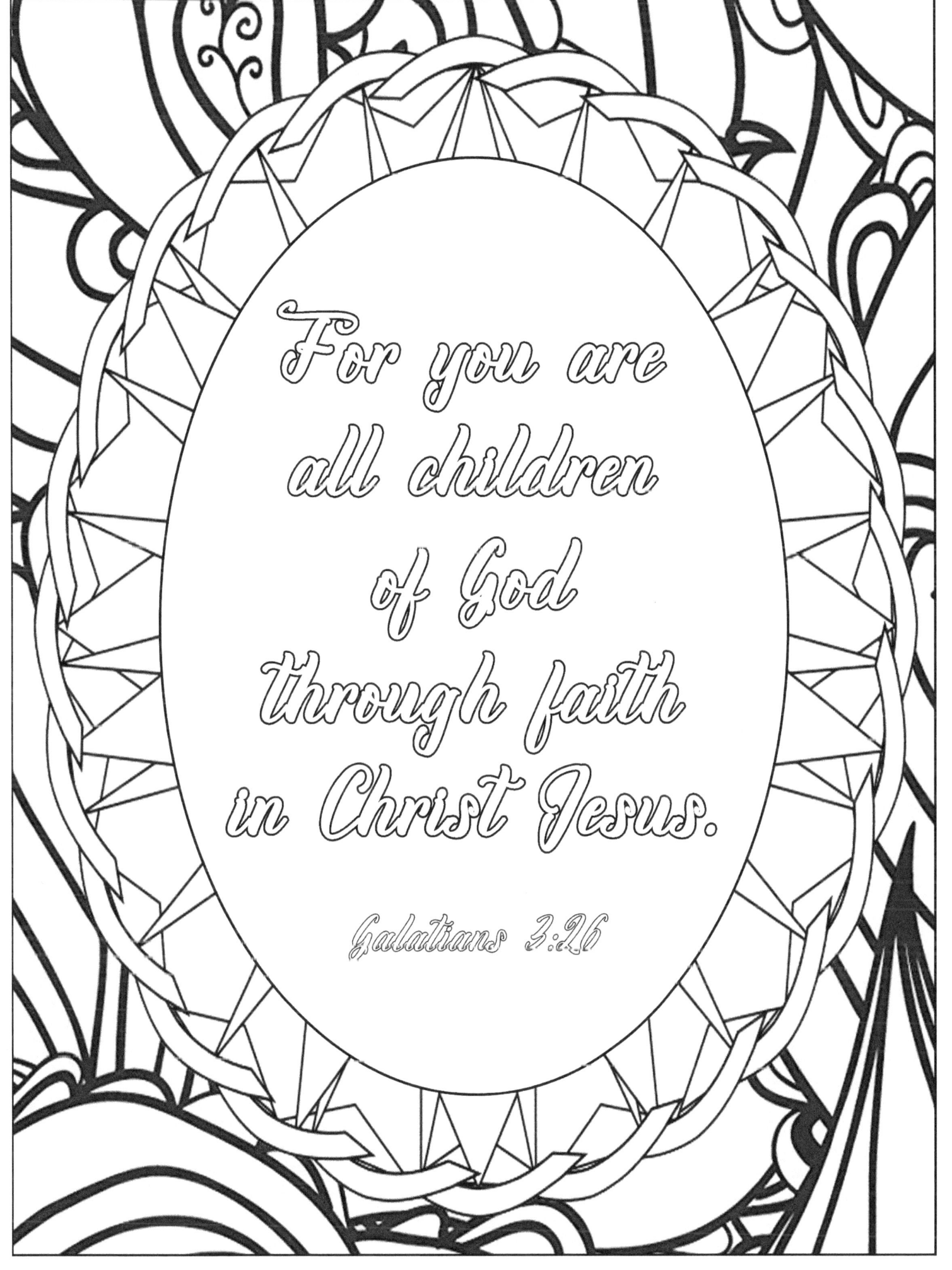

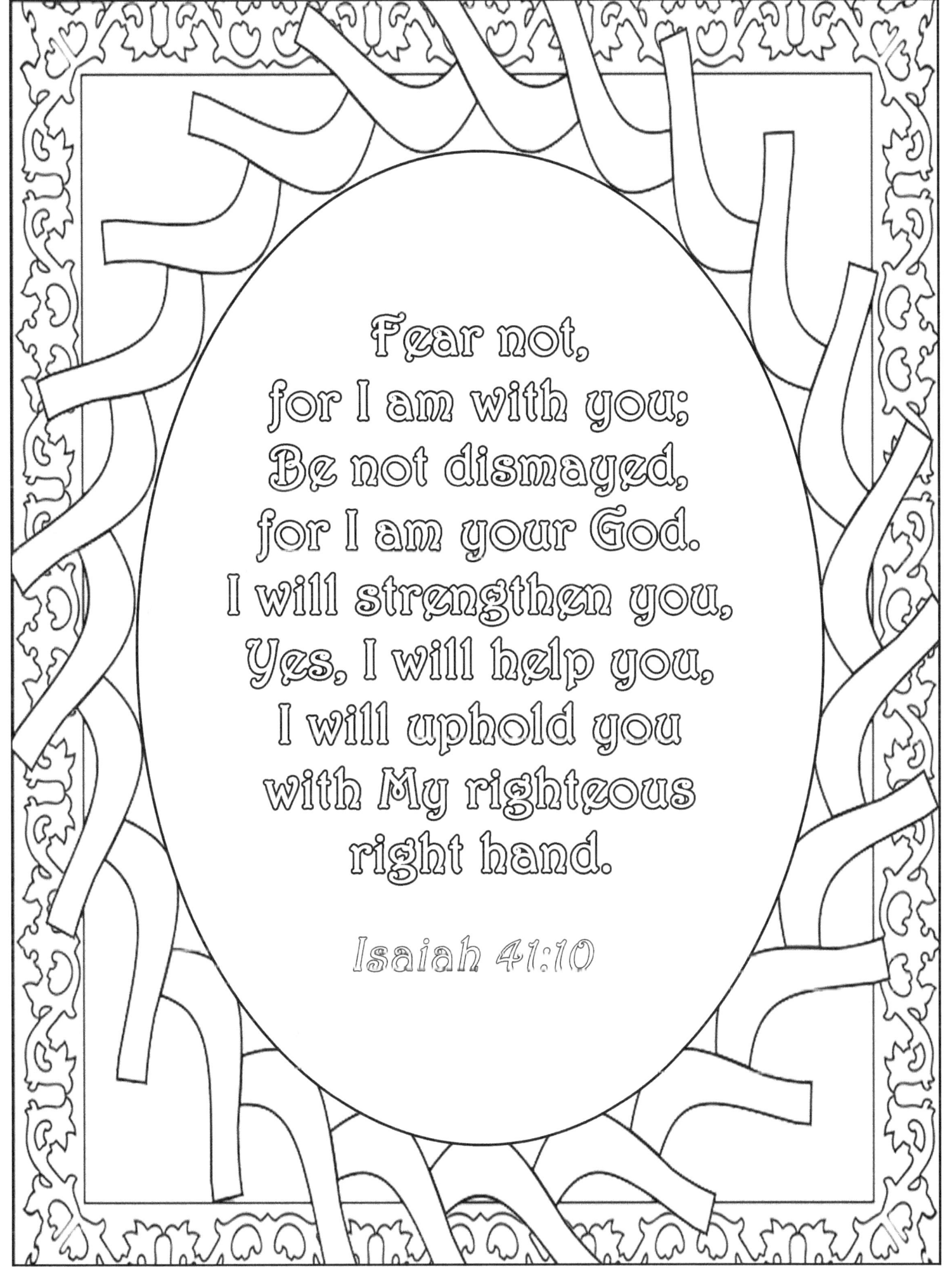

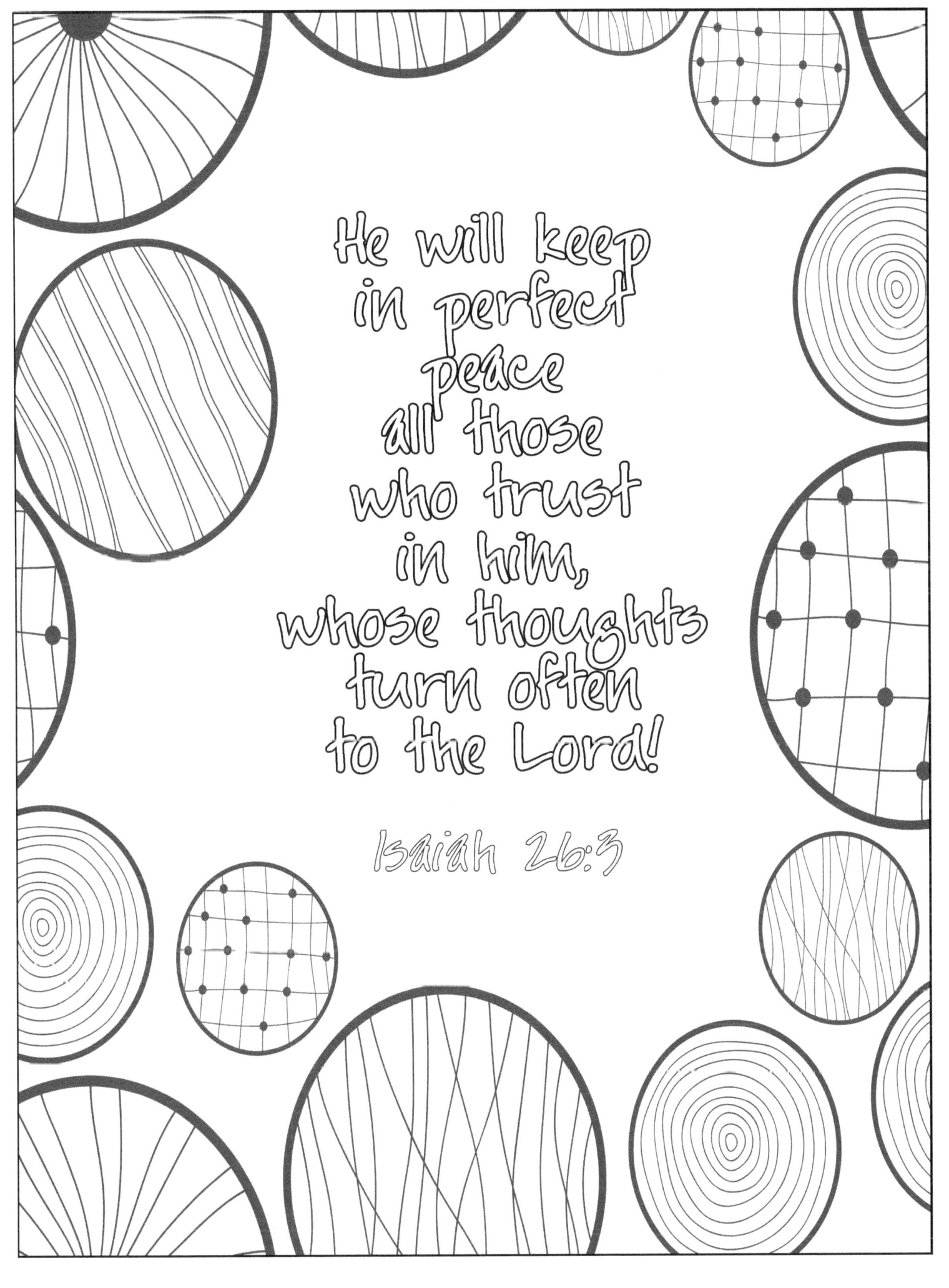

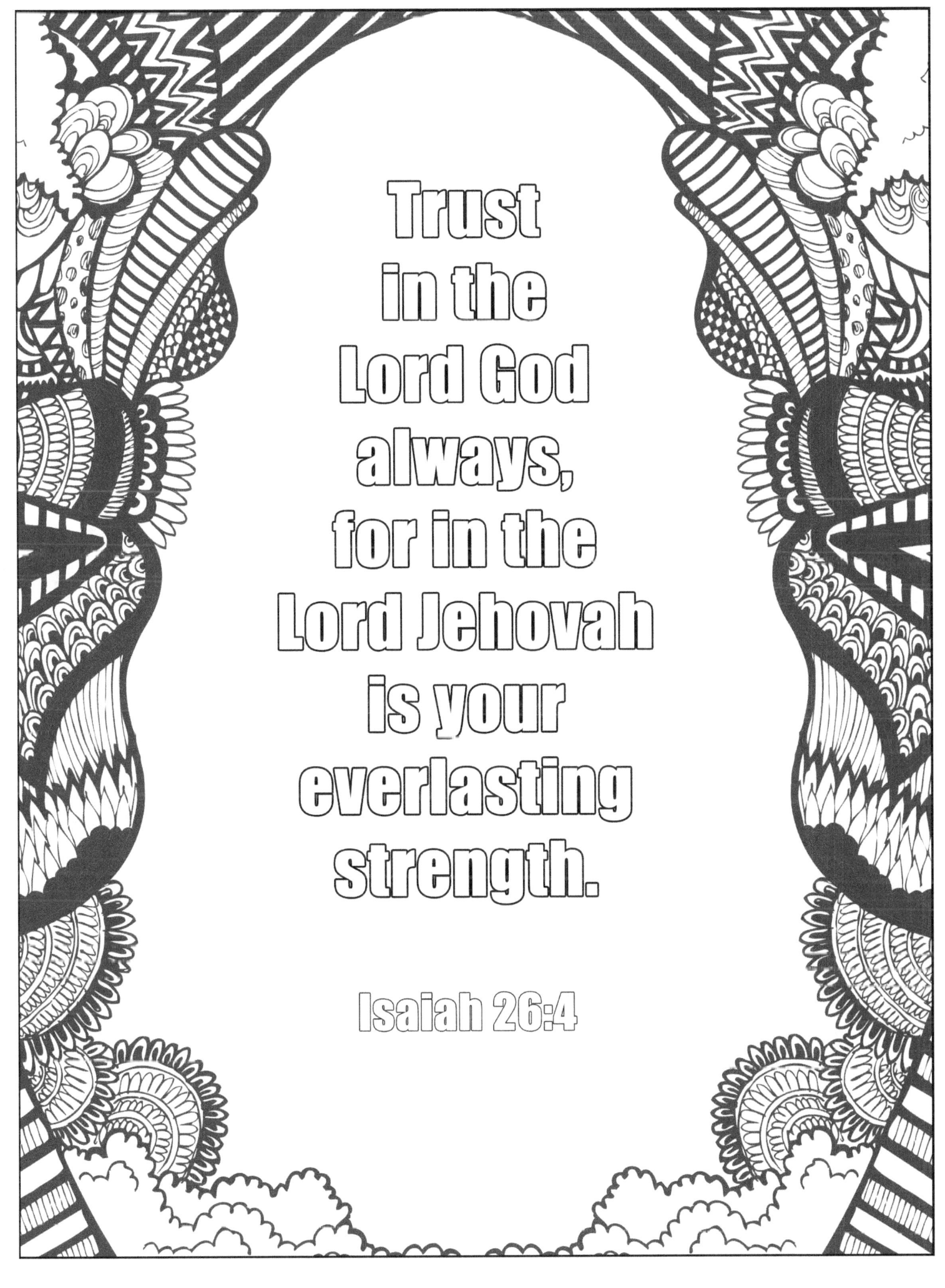

Trust in the Lord God always, for in the Lord Jehovah is your everlasting strength.

Isaiah 26:4

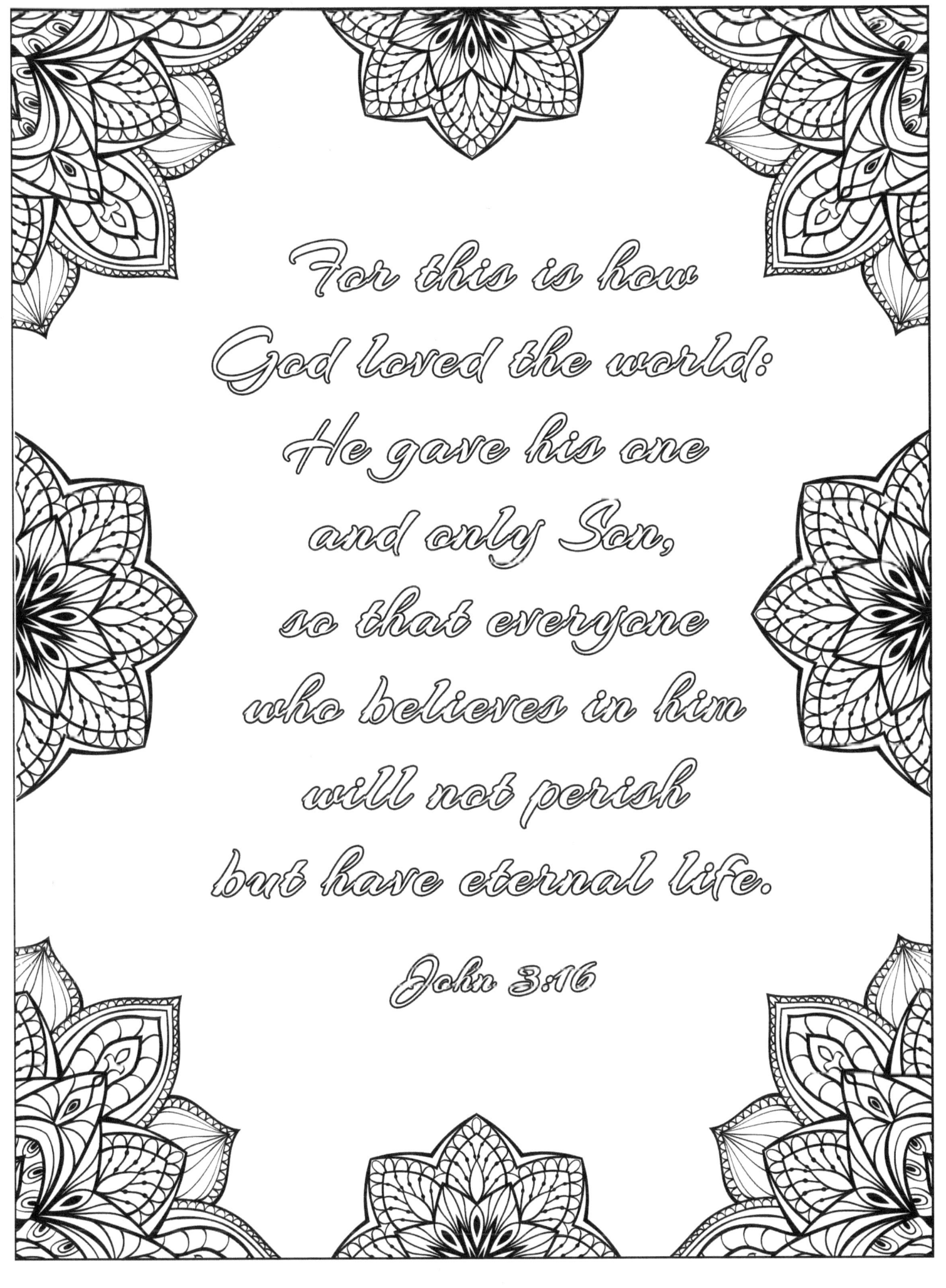

Color Test Page

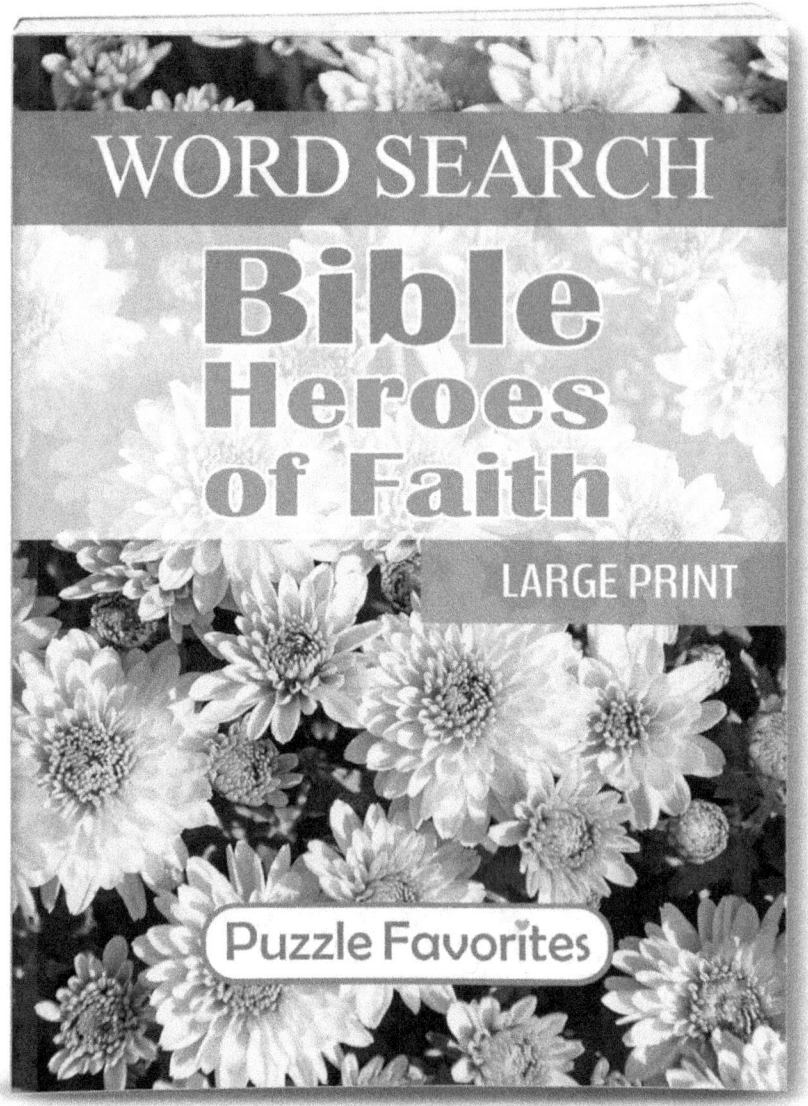

WORD SEARCH

Bible
Heroes
of Faith

LARGE PRINT

Puzzle Favorites

ISBN: 978-1983502743

Amazon: 198350274X

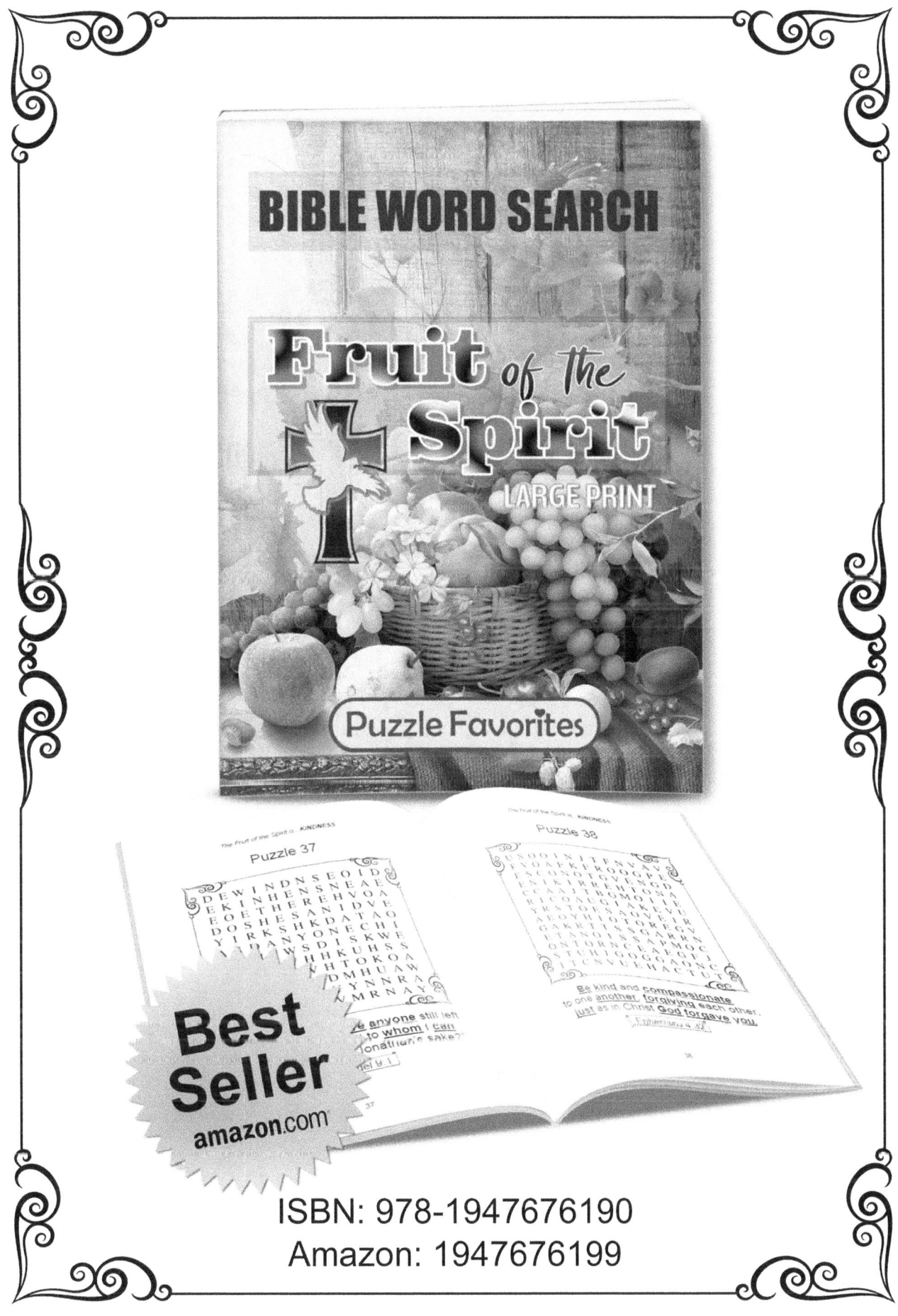

ISBN: 978-1947676190
Amazon: 1947676199

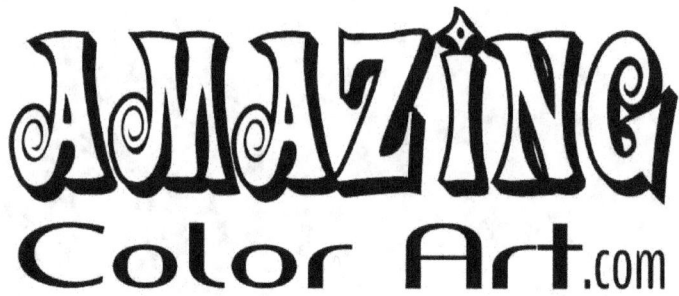

Amazing
Media Works
Print and Digital Publishing
www.AmazingMediaWorks.com

All images licensed and/or used with permission

Enjoy these great titles and more by Amazing Color Art!

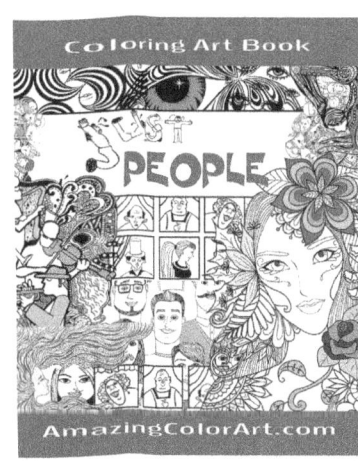

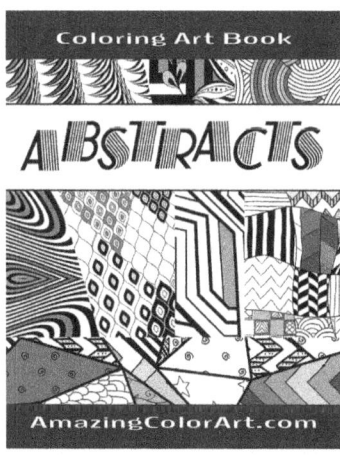

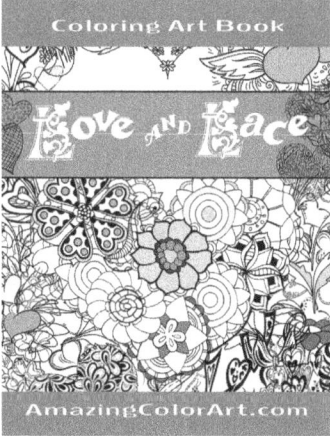

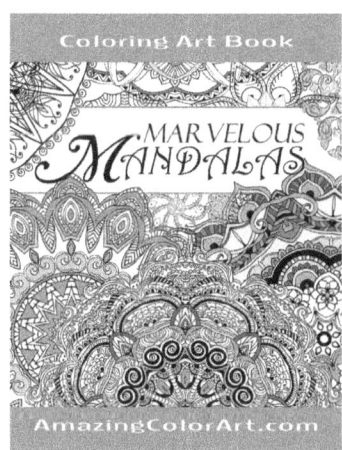

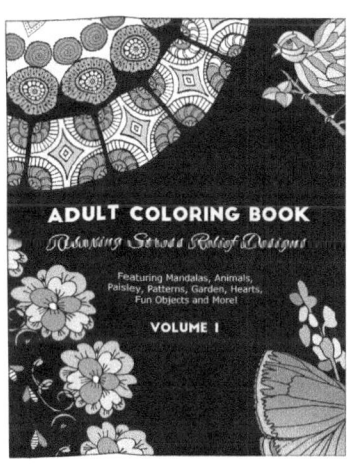

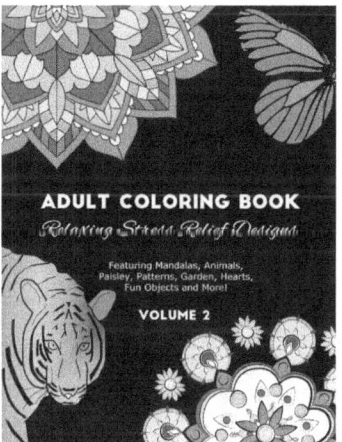

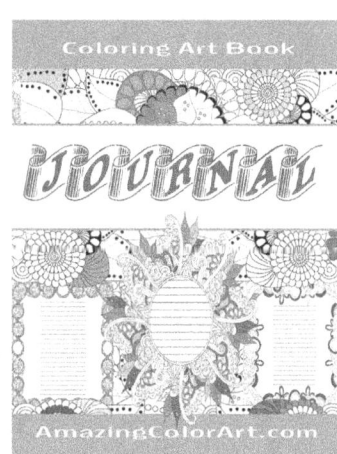

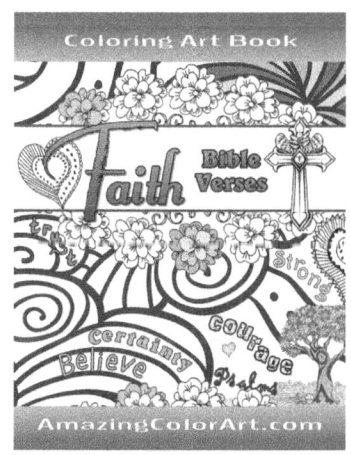

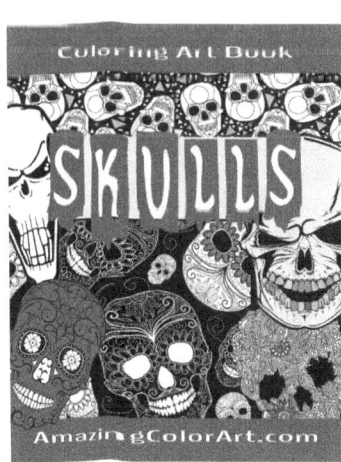

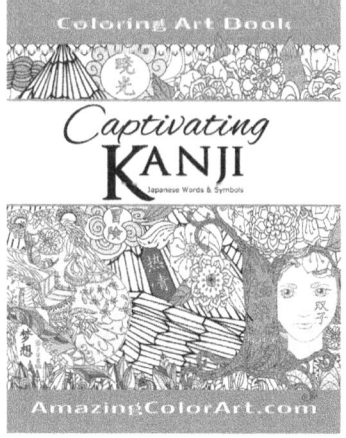

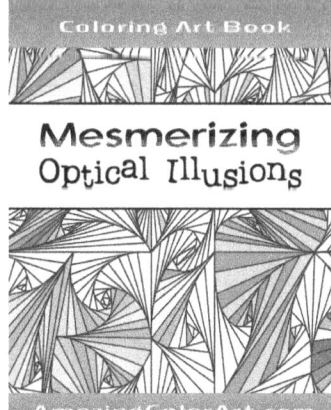

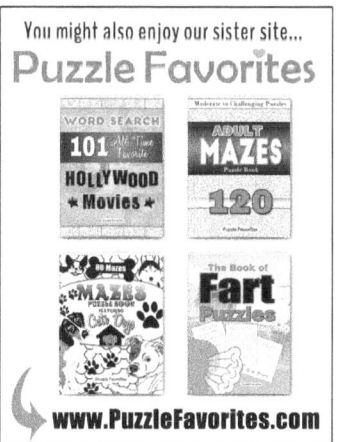